Fixing You is Killing Me

A CONSCIOUS ROADMAP TO KNOWING WHEN TO SAVE AND WHEN TO LEAVE YOUR RELATIONSHIP

Stuart Motola

Crescendo
PUBLISHING

Fixing You is Killing Me: A Conscious Roadmap to Knowing When to Save and When to Leave Your Relationship
By Stuart Motola

Crescendo Publishing, LLC
2-558 Upper Gage Ave., Ste. 246
Hamilton, ON L8V 4J6
Canada

GetPublished@CrescendoPublishing.com
1-877-575-8814

ISBN: 978-1-948719-04-9 (p)
ISBN: 978-1-948719-05-6 (e)

Printed in the United States of America
Cover design by XXX

10 9 8 7 6 5 4 3 2 1

Message from the Author

Ideas are powerful. They can change the world. But true change happens with action. Don't just read the book. Put it into action. Hear a special message from Stuart and/or download the free Action Workbook at: www.stuartmotola.com/fixingyou-action

One more thing, community amplifies action. Share your path with us. We grow faster and stronger together. Join our online community of readers at: www.stuartmotola.com/community

Endorsements

"Stuart takes us beyond the binary of 'I'm done' or 'I love him' and into the space between the two. We emerge with a model of love that doesn't depend on the sacrifice of the self to be made valid, but rather one that comes alive as we do. Read this if you've come to the edge of a relationship and aren't sure whether to step forward or back. Either way it will help you to move into something new and bigger."

Maddie Berky,
Food, Sex, & Worthiness Writer and Coach

"This important and insightful book offers enormous hope to couples. It presents a fresh path forward during that painful time in so many relationships where partners may be questioning everything. Stuart shows you how to navigate a powerful path and happy ending through the gut wrenching questions, doubt and consequences involved in making the decision to stay or go."

Tommi Wolfe,
CEO, Top 6 Business Coach

"Stuart shares a powerful story of love, uncertainty, sadness and, ultimately, triumph over shame and fear. He models the growth and maturity required to navigate one of life's hardest challenges within a committed relationship. And his careful, caring way of telling his story models the conscious, empathetic and loving decisions he made throughout his journey. I highly recommend this book to anyone who wants to learn how to handle the inevitable discomfort and struggles we all face in our committed relationships."

Steve Horsmon,
Men's Coach, Goodguys2Greatmen

"Stuart has written a powerful book that reflects his passion, knowledge and commitment to the transformation possible in committed relationship. This insightful book is an exceptional resource to help us create an authentic life."

Nick Meima,
After Divorce Support Coach

Table of Contents

Dedication

Dedicated to my son, Julien. Not a day goes by when I am not grateful for you. You are a constant light in my life. Always remember, we can all be heroes.

"Self-deception denies reality. But when the pain grows great enough, reality insists on breaking through."

– Willard and Marguerite Beecher, *Beyond Success and Failure*

Preface

This is a book about the holy grail of ever-elusive happiness in long-term relationship. To have struggled in relationship is to be human. It happens to everyone. At its best, we grow wiser and happier, and rise up from struggle. At its worst, we find ourselves asking, *Is this it? This one person for the rest of my life?* Often a barrage of other questions ensues. *Do we even love each other still? Could I live without her? Could I be happy without him?*

Like hornets buzzing around one's head, these questions can be relentless and incredibly exasperating. Often, they push us to the precipice of a major life change. We find ourselves at the edge of a cliff, uncertain whether to take the leap or stay where we are. This book is written to help you determine if a) you are at the precipice, and b) you are ready to take the leap. The leap is different for everyone; it is not just about leaving your relationship. Sometimes it's about reinventing who you are with your partner. You will also find in this book guidance on how to make the leap in the most graceful way possible, how to land, and where to go from there.

Relationship challenges offer us a remarkable opportunity to grow and define what we want with a partner. How can we best meet those challenges to come out bigger and stronger? I offer you stories and insights on how to do just that—to arrive at a place where you trust yourself to act. It is a place of your own power and inner authority, aligned with who you are and what you want in your life and relationship.

I write from the authority of having taken the leap. I was in a twenty-year marriage in which I had lost who I was. I fell apart entirely to rebuild myself—a personal story that I will share, as well as client stories and the universal insights I learned. To be clear, I'm not a psychotherapist, psychologist, sociologist, or mythologist. I love those disciplines, study them passionately, and stand on the shoulders of giants in those fields. I coach individuals on how to transform their lives and grow strong when relationship challenges arise, particularly when the "save it or leave it" question comes up.

I lived a certain path in life, descended to my own personal ground zero, and emerged stronger. I support others with the journey I have taken. I've studied my own situation deeply and synthesized the wisdom of great thinkers and teachers with my own experience. There's a common humanity to my story that runs parallel to my clients' lives.

"From the rat wheel to a place of power and intention," one client said recently.

Yes, relationship or anything we do unquestioningly without clarity can feel like a rat wheel. How do we get back to our power and intention? My hope is that in reading ahead, you will gain many insights on how to do this, for the transformation of yourself and the ones you love.

Disclaimer

To protect the privacy of the persons mentioned in the pages ahead, the names of family members and clients have been changed. For non-heterosexual couples, please insert the appropriate pronoun as appropriate for you in the text ahead. And lastly, if you are in an abusive relationship and fear for your safety, action items from this book may not apply to you. Though the necessity to leave your relationship may be imminent, proceed with caution and reach out for help as necessary. Call the national abuse hotline at: 1-800-799-SAFE

Chapter 1

Setting Emancipatory Grounds

*"Emancipate yourselves from mental slavery.
None but ourselves can free our minds."*

– Marcus Garvey, sung by Bob Marley in *Redemption Song*

I'm done. The words kept repeating in my mind. I feared them, but they still came. I sat alone on the edge of my canopied king size bed. If I acted, everything would be blown apart—a twenty-year marriage, a home of fifteen years, the relationship with my fifteen-year-old son, and a family business of twenty-one years. If I didn't act, the lie would continue. At forty-five, my life had come down to two words.

I could barely eat, sleep, or work. I struggled to be in bed at night next to my wife. I burned inside with turmoil at the dinner table. I tried to ignore it. How could I trust this voice? How could I betray my family? And yet, how could I deny its truth?

The landscape split open, a daunting cliff appeared, and I looked down. Below was the unknown and frightening future, and also the excitement of change—a chance to get out. I considered the leap, heart racing. Jump or play it safe?

The threshold. The moment of no return. The crossing over.

We all come to such a moment in our lives. Our primary relationship is suddenly no longer sustainable. We struggle to stay engaged in it and simultaneously can't fathom getting out. Our partner offers us safety and refuge from loneliness. The benefits of making a change may not outweigh the costs. And yet a demanding voice inside tells us something's got to change. Some movement besides the same old, same old is required. Our entire system, mind, body, and soul say so. We struggle to show up in life, we are at a crossroads, and we must do something. But what?

Emancipate? Yes! Free ourselves from the confinement, enslavement, or prison. Enter a new landscape of possibilities. Get out of the jail we've sculpted for ourselves of who we've become.

Who holds the key? It is within us, is it not? In our minds, our logic, our fears. Our relationship with our selves forms the prison cell. The bars that confine us are the lies we tell ourselves to avoid change. How do we break free from the fear-based stories? How do we emancipate from the lies? And why did this prison get built in the first place?

The Beginning of Love

Two decades before the words *I'm done* kept reverberating in my mind, I met my great young love at a party in San Francisco. I was twenty-two; she was twenty. She was with another guy—the classic drunk poet. She had long, flowing brown hair, a tightly-fitted blouse and hip-hugging skirt, and I was immediately attracted to her. She was smart, articulate, and charismatic. I was heady, arrogant, and buff, having just come off a summer of leading kids on canoe trips in the Upper Peninsula of Michigan, portaging seventy-five-pound aluminum canoes four miles at a time. Throughout the party that night, I pursued her in brief exchanges with witty playful conversation. As I left, I found her one last time and kissed her. She was amused.

On our first date a week later, the conversation was lacking over dinner. It was clear we were both bored. Something needed to shift.

"Let's get out of here," I said. We crossed the street, went back to my shared apartment, and climbed the four floors to the roof that overlooked the Mission district. The night, sprinkled with city lights, sparked another avenue of connection. I rested my hands on her shoulders and touched my lips to hers.

On our second date, we went skinny-dipping at Gray Whale Beach in Pacifica, cold waters just south of San Francisco. I was awed at her physical confidence. Before I even said, "Let's go for a swim," she took off all her clothes and jumped into the ocean.

Six weeks later, after occasional visits, she asked me to drive her home from San Francisco to Berkeley. I knew she was seeing several men at the time. I asked her, "Am I just another clown in your circus?" Years later, she would say that was her *you got me* moment: "No guy had ever been that direct with me before."

We spent the next few months playing and frolicking on the Northern California coast in Indian Summer. She was unemployed. I was barely employed. Freedom was everything. Within six months, we moved in together. A year and a half later, we travelled the Northwest for three months looking for a new place to call home, in a VW bus we bought at a police auction. We visited Oregon, the Olympic Peninsula, San Juan Islands, British Colombia, Hornsby Island, Glacier National Park, Idaho, and Montana, among other places. We experimented with mushrooms. We made art. She directed plays. I wrote fiction.

Over the years, we watched each other work hard to become responsible adults giving our gifts to the world. I was a passionate teacher and writer. She was a theater artist. We were very much in love.

We had the idea of The One, the partner who would complete us. I wanted to make her happy and took it on as my manly duty. I would gladly sacrifice my needs for hers. She was everything to me. I could abandon myself to her lovingly. I was young, naïve, idealistic, and stubborn. I was in love.

And I was betraying myself.

Self-Betrayal

Self-betrayal is acting against one's own interests and well-being. It's a simple yet confusing concept. Why would anyone act against his or her own self interests? Don't our survival instincts guard against it? Yes and no. The circumstances of self-betrayal are complicated. People betray themselves every day without even knowing it. Unconsciously, millions of us do it. In relationship, it's self-abandonment. I'd rather lose a part of me so I do not lose a part of you. It was my script and one that many people follow.

We self-betray in order to get love and avoid losing it. We self-betray to avoid tough situations and painful truths. We do it to stay safe. If I don't upset her, she'll love me. If I stay at my job, everything will work itself out. I can only be complete through you. She sees me like no one else. Any time we ignore our own needs, we are self-betraying. It is a way of not dealing with reality. It's how we play small. It is how we avoid change and stay stuck in old ways that no longer serve us.

Just Gas and the Rescuer

When I met my wife Marisa, I thought that to be a man was to make my woman happy. If you had told me back then that she was responsible for her own happiness, I would have understood the concept and nodded, but my actions would not have changed. What purpose did I serve in her life, if not to make her happy?

I will make you happy, baby, was my mantra.

Others saw it. My family spoke of it. My friends implied it—but none of it reached me. I was certain love would make everything okay. I believed it with all my heart. She was a beautiful person who completed me, and who I could complete. She gave me purpose, passion, and life. I could put my energy into her. Unconsciously, I was avoiding myself.

Five years after first meeting in San Francisco, we got married in a small, village-style wedding at an Inn on East Pearl Street in Boulder, Colorado. Three years later, we had a son. Ten days after his birth, I turned thirty. I was barely making a living as a teacher, unsure how I would meet the demands of my new life.

Beyond financial challenges, there was also lots of illness. My infant son had recurring croup coughs that would last for hours on end until we ended up in the ER. For three and a half years, we dealt with the croup—until finally he was diagnosed with viral asthma and we got a handle on it with a nebulizer. Health issues also began cropping up with Marisa, which also landed us in the ER three times in less than two years. I recall one night, I was slumped alone on the steps in our home while everyone was asleep, crying and calling out to God (I was not religious at all): "Why is everyone in my family sick so much?" Several nights later, we were in the emergency room yet again.

The fluorescent lights were deathly bright for two in the morning. My three-year-old son was asleep on my lap. I struggled to stay awake, mustering all my energy to soothe my wife, who was in terrible pain. Another belly attack. We'd had many of these over the years, the first when we were together only six months. I remember I'd spent the evening rubbing her stomach, tending to her with tea in a friend's apartment in the Haight district.

The doctor ripped open the sheet along the tracks of our curtained cubicle. I was hoping he'd tell us something substantial, an actual diagnosis—nothing too bad, of course. The prior visits had yielded nothing. Just gas, they'd told us. Both times had cost $1,000, the two enemas, $2,000. I was stressed about another big bill. I looked into the doctor's eyes, hoping to make a connection. He was young, maybe my age, but he didn't receive my gaze—seemingly bored with his job. *Please don't tell me it's gas again*, I thought.

"Well, the good news is…" he began.

I knew what was coming. I threw up my hands. Was there a God? I couldn't stand all this suffering with no answers anymore.

"…the antacid we gave her seems to be making her better. She's terribly impacted."

I know, doc, she's all blocked up. Enough, I thought. *Let's get out of here. This is the last time,* I told myself, *the last time I'm taking her to the ER.*

This was one of a string of incidents over the years. I don't mean to make light of her pain or imply that my wife didn't have serious health concerns. Gas, while it may sound like a minor thing, can cause severe distress. The actual diagnosis that we came to, many years later, was Irritable Bowel Syndrome (IBS). Millions of people go to the ER every year because of it. In worst-case scenarios, an individual can suffer such bad intestinal obstruction that she could die without medical attention. What came to be discovered over the years was not just IBS, but also gallbladder disease, as well as a host of other medically tough to treat conditions like candida, chronic fatigue syndrome, low t-killer cells, auto immune deficiency, and West Nile Virus, to name a few.

At the time, however, we endured years of alternative doctor bills, failed diagnoses and few effective solutions. This added up to $35,000 a year in medical bills—and eventually, bankruptcy. Worse was my feeling of inner bankruptcy, my sense that I was failing her. I felt impotent from my inability to help my wife get well. I was doing all I could—making dinners, doing the food shopping and laundry, driving our son to and from school, running our demanding business, managing family finances, and more—trying to give her the space to heal. Many years into our marriage, I couldn't keep up with it all. When someone asked me what was going on with my wife, I often said, "I don't know." I had mentally checked out by then. My beautiful wife was becoming invisible to me.

As the medical bills piled up, I sought to limit expenses while we tried many alternative therapies to heal her, including electrical therapy to zap candida bacteria and countless supplements that insurance would never cover. She was able to function at work and in the world, but always had something going on—a cold, a pain, aches, fatigue, dizziness. I felt her every pain and ache in my heart. I thought that was love.

With insufficient concern for my own well-being, I based my own success on the happiness of my wife and family. Like many parents today, I was burning the candle at both ends. At my own peril, I did not practice much self-care, and really didn't know what that meant. Except for rare occasions, I sacrificed my own passions to be with my wife and son even though I felt like a prisoner. I spent all of my time with them; I needed time for myself, but was afraid to ask for it. My wife demanded a lot of me and I complied. A voice in my head said, *You can't leave them, leave her alone with Jake for the entire day. She's not well. What kind of husband are you? What kind of father?*

I was living "the dream" of today's all-consuming family life. Alienated from the larger breathing apparatus of extended family and a community, like many mothers and fathers I work with in my coaching practice, I felt stifled. We focus on being "good men and women," who want to do it better than our parents did by being present for our families. We do our best to be good to our wives and husbands, good to our families, good to our children—good men and women in the eyes of society. Yet, often, we're miserable and running ourselves ragged. While being good to everyone else, we are no longer true to ourselves and pay the price.

I was stuck in the role of Rescuer/Martyr, sacrificing myself at the altar of my wife's illness, slowly eaten up with bitterness. Consumed in my own self-betrayal, not knowing my own needs, it took me years to break free.

Life's a Bitch: Sacrificing Self, a Bad Way to Live

Growing up as a kid in the 70s in suburban New York, self-betrayal was everywhere. I remember as a kid, adults often said, "Life's a bitch. You pay taxes, then you die." It was as if the rules of life were irreversibly written. Go to work, do your job, tolerate your spouse, put up with the kids, and die. As a child, I knew something was wrong. Invisible to me, the lives of adults were blowing up with adultery, alcoholism, drug abuse, and tax evasion.

Nonetheless, as an adult, I dutifully continued the cycle of self-betrayal as the marker of the right way to live. I sacrificed my interests in music, writing, and the outdoors to be fully available for my family. In my marriage, I gave up passion for security. Love for safety. Vitality for approval. And soon enough, it caught up to me.

Self-sacrifice is honorable, but it has a clear cost. Yes, there's integrity and honor in paying the bills, keeping the family afloat and the marriage alive. But how do we know when it crosses into self-betrayal? Simply put, we begin to feel dead inside.

Day in and day out, I went to work, checked off tasks, and kept up with errands, not knowing what the doing was truly for—beyond paying the bills to keep a roof over our heads. I no longer knew what I was really working for. I had lost my imagination for how I could be engaged in my relationship or show up at our business in a more fulfilling way. I had mentally and emotionally checked out, and fallen into a survival pattern. I felt the loss of my life force—dreams buried, just barely getting by. My family got an exhausted, stressed-out version of myself. This was not noble. This was insanity. It was self-betrayal, ensconced in a pattern that is ravaging marriages and families today like never before.

Are you on auto pilot? Or are you living your dream—loving your family, work, and life? At all times, we must challenge self-sacrifice with self-honoring. We must ask, what does it mean to thrive? We must challenge the myth that living honorably means endless doing and self-sacrifice for others. When our good intentions to care for others become unhealthy, it is known in social psychology as "pathological altruism." Even if what we are doing is just and moral, if we are doing it for the wrong reasons, it causes harm to ourselves and those we wish to serve. I don't buy into the story that having a dream and vision of one's own is selfish. Far from being selfish, it is a great gift to you, your partner, and your family. A vital and energized you, who gives the best of you to others—that is your truest gift in this life.

My Soul Is from Somewhere Else

"All day I think about it, then at night I say it.
Where did I come from, and what am I supposed to be doing?
I have no idea.
My soul is from elsewhere, I'm sure of that,
And I intend to end up there."

– Rumi, *Who Says Words with My Mouth?*

The poet knows something is not right. He does not know what he is "supposed to be doing." He's not on track with his soul but he knows he needs to end up where his soul is. The knowledge of separation from one's soul is the seed of the Initiatory Journey, often referred to as midlife crisis—that moment when you know something's just not right. And from there, the questions ensue.

- Is this all there is to life?
- Have I wasted my life with this person?
- Have I been checked out, asleep in my life?
- Am I living a lie?
- Am I sculpting my life in a way that honors my highest priorities?

All are big questions challenging patterns of self-betrayal. When you ask them, you are waking up.

Unwiring Myself

Always committed to self-inquiry, I spent the better part of my twenties in sweat lodges, sun dances, and vision fasts. At thirty, with a son just born and terrified at the new financial and personal responsibility, I went into therapy. I was fortunate to find a great therapist. He was an international trainer of therapists in a cutting-edge, psychosomatic approach. He was generous and agreed to see me on a sliding scale. His kindness touched me at a pivotal time of my life.

The birth of our son, Jake, had changed everything. Marisa and I could no longer be everything for one another. Our old pattern of co-regulating (making each other okay) was severely disrupted. Our relationship was fracturing. Clearly, we could no longer keep it up— but we did not know otherwise. While happy at times, stresses built up. Overwhelm, chronic illness, too much to do, and mutual invisibility ran rampant. We had lost one another and our marriage could no longer hold all that it once had.

Over the next decade throughout my thirties, I did a lot of personal growth work. I worked with multiple life coaches and attended many retreats, focused on developing healthy masculinity. I was determined to unwire and reconfigure myself to find a way into a healthy relationship with myself and my wife. I believed I could always do better. Even in the face of daunting demands, I was a stressed-out optimist. And over the years, I became acutely aware that the enmeshed dynamic with my wife came from my own feelings of inadequacy, low self-esteem, and self-betrayal.

How Did I Get Here?

Eleven years later, after the ER moment, the lining began to tear for real. I had struggled over the years, but action called on me to make a change. I was forty-four. My wife and I were planning a family trip. To California, of course. We always went to California. She believed herself healthier near the ocean. I was sick of California.

"I want to go somewhere else," I said with some hesitance, fearful of conflict.

"So, where then? Where do you want to go?" she responded.

"I don't know. Alaska, the Northwest."

"I can't swim there. You know I need the ocean," she said. "That's my sacrifice for living in Colorado. I need my ocean time."

Your sacrifice? I thought. *My whole life with you is a sacrifice.*

"So, it's California or nothing?" I said.

"You get your mountains. I get my ocean and beach time," she said. "I feel better there. It's where I come alive. It's my healing place."

Out of love, I had resigned my life to being in the passenger seat of her life. In service to her wellness, I'd given her the steering wheel of our life. Most of our choices were driven by her health, her needs, and her desires. Multiple nights per week, after a long day at work, I prepared whole meals with protein, vegetables, and starch; simple soup and grilled cheese would not suffice. Meals out had to be fish or sushi. No red meat, pasta, gluten, or dairy. Days out were in town or in the city, as the mountain altitude was too much for her sinuses.

If I didn't meet her needs, she told me something that crushed me. Eight words that had the power to pulverize everything I had devoted my life to. And at least once every few months, she delivered them:

"I don't feel like you're on my team."

Not on your team? Of course I'm on your team. Everything I do is to be on your team. I couldn't hear it. I loved her greatly. I wanted to make her happy. I wanted to help her heal physically, to help her heal from her past.

Growing up, neither of her parents had been a solid presence. Her mother could be engaged and magical in one moment and vindictive and terrorizing in the next. Consistent instability, apartment evictions, rent not being paid, volatility, and a lack of safety had marked my wife's childhood. At twelve years old, she had been told by her mother to no longer call her mom but Mousey. A few years later, her mother had ended up homeless on the streets of Manhattan. As a teenager, my wife had walked to school hoping to avoid seeing her mother, who had become the Bag Lady in Central Park. Her mother was an undiagnosed schizophrenic. What my wife had been through broke my heart.

It angered me to no end that her father had not taken control of the situation. He was a talented photographer who shot the covers of *Life Magazine* in the late sixties, but he was not a forceful person. As a teenager, Marisa had shared an Upper East Side apartment with him, essentially taking care of herself. By eighteen, she'd worked full time, managing a real estate office. At twenty, she'd left New York for San Francisco.

Marisa had extricated herself from a tough upbringing at a young age. That took tremendous courage. She was super talented and started one of the most successful companies in her field. With my tenacity on the business side, the company grew to new heights. In my mind, what was more important than the business success was the stable, family structure she was able to settle into and trust. I felt such pride in having supported her in that way. And I feared failing her the way her parents had.

In the process, I'd sacrificed my needs, wishes, and desires. When I attempted to communicate my challenges, it blew up on me. She was averse to conflict, and got defensive and scared. I got angry and helpless. To reign me in, all she had to do was deliver the eight words I dreaded hearing: "I don't feel like you're on my team." Logically, the accusation made no sense—but it got in. *What good is a man if he's not on his wife's team?* I wondered. And then I got back in line, trying to be the man she needed me to be.

Looking into her brown eyes in the dining room of our suburban house that day, I knew where things would go if I continued to push against her desire to go to California. I could not bring up how Amtrak was three times the cost of flying. How could I be so heartless? She had inner ear problems and a fear of flying. I did not want to be accused of being callous about her well-being. After more than a decade of this dynamic, I felt like I was dying inside.

It's her vacation, not mine, I told myself, rationalizing my avoidance of the impasse I knew awaited me if I objected. I left the room and went upstairs. I sat on the edge of our canopy bed, her dream bed, in the high-ceilinged bedroom, her dream bedroom. The adjoining master bathroom and giant tub, all that was more hers than mine.

"This is my house!" she had screamed within seconds of walking in for the first time, several years earlier.

And there I was, on her dream bed in her dream house, living the lyrics of The Talking Heads song, "Once in a Lifetime":

> *And you may find yourself in a beautiful house*
> *With a beautiful wife*
> *And you may ask yourself, well*
> *How did I get here?*

I sat blank for several seconds, shocked and stunned, in a state of disbelief. I considered all that I was doing: running a successful business, being a "good man," stepping up for my wife and family.

How *DID* I get here?

I had slipped into pathological altruism and forgotten my dreams. I didn't even know what they were anymore. I felt hollow in the pit of my stomach. Something was terribly wrong with how I had navigated my life. How could this be?

Chapter 2

The Call and the Initiatory Journey

*"In the middle of the journey of our life I came to myself
within a dark wood where the straight way was lost."*

– Dante Alighieri, *Inferno, Canto I*

Whether we like it or not, it comes for most of us—the dark wood, the crisis, the initiatory event, the Awakening, the Hero's Journey. It happens often in midlife. A fifty-two-year-old man sleeps with a twenty-two-year-old woman. A straight-laced guy buys a Harley Davidson. A forty-eight-year-old woman goes skydiving. Call it a crack in the seam of life. One's entire sense of purpose falls away and the energy to keep showing up is lost. In my thirties, I thought, *Oh no, that will never happen to me, I'm way too on top of my game.* But it happened anyway.

Clearly, my old life was no longer working. Something had to change. Something was breaking. I had met my wife as a twenty-two-year-old boy and married five years later. For years, we orbited around each other. We were everything to one another. We had a deep dependency on each other for our identity and were profoundly enmeshed. We had few friends outside of our relationship and did everything together. We were primary and secondary to one another. As the years passed, a child was born and life's demands augmented. Finally, I had arrived, terrified, looking over the cliff of my life.

The Risk It Takes to Blossom

*"The day came when the risk to remain tight in a bud
was more painful than the risk it took to blossom."*

– Anais Nin, Author

The Initiatory Journey is life-rupturing. It breaks us open, and brings us to the moment of which Anais Nin speaks. You may be there right now. Or you may feel inklings of it. It's as if somebody is knocking at the door of your life saying, "Come, it's time to go—time to enter your new life."

This is the new life cracking open. Life's cosmic forces are kicking your ass into the next part of your life. It may show up as a marriage that's dying or a job that's killing you. Whatever the source, it's the prison you've built, a monument to safety and the status quo. Suddenly, the veil has been lifted. Your soul says, "No more. Something's got to change."

Of course, many of us try to shut it down, stuff ourselves back into the box of our functioning life, go to work, stay safe, tolerate a partner, or check out altogether—anything to keep the ship afloat. We refuse the call for change. As we learn to recognize the meaning of this cracking open—to know the life of our soul—we accept the rupture as an opportunity. Our genius is calling on us to realign our lives toward something greater and more vital for ourselves, our families, and humanity.

Initiation

*"It has always been the prime function of mythology and rite
to supply the symbols that carry the human spirit forward, in
counteraction to those other constant human fantasies that tend
to tie it back ... We remain fixated to the unexorcised images of
our infancy, and hence disinclined to the necessary passages of our*

adulthood … In the United States there is even a pathos of inverted emphasis: the goal is not to grow old but to remain young."

– Joseph Campbell, *The Hero with a Thousand Faces*

To initiate is to grow—grow up, grow old, and grow wise—to move toward a new stage of life. Traditionally, initiation describes the rite of passage of children into adulthood. Yet today, we have many adults who are but children inside, never initiated into adulthood. Maybe they got a driver's license, went through a high school graduation ceremony, or got married. It didn't meaningfully transform them into adults. In the void of meaning, young people attempt to initiate themselves—through sex, drugs, and risky behavior. As a result, we have many uninitiated adults making important decisions with the inner compass of a child.

In midlife, typically between thirty-five and sixty, a second chance at initiation comes to us. Some of us revert back to adolescent activities like sleeping around recklessly and overusing drugs. Others commit unthinkable harm to loved ones. This behavior occurs because, as Campbell says, we don't have a mythology or rite to carry us forward. We have no structure to hold us during this time of rupture. To supply such a forwarding structure is one of my primary goals in my work. To articulate a roadmap from which we may leverage crisis into growth and mature adulthood. In crisis, we have the opportunity to grow and enter a new vision of life. With successful passage, we may become healthy mature adults, emancipated into the second half of our lives.

Initiation as a rite of passage was first studied in academia by the German-born French ethnographer, Charles-Arnold Kurr van Gennep, in the early 1900s in Holland. Gennep travelled extensively to tribal communities throughout South America to study initiatory practices. He discovered three explicit stages of Initiation: Separation, Liminality, and Incorporation. The first step is to separate from the old life. Liminality speaks to the moving into the unknown, the "in-between" space. Incorporation refers to bringing back gifts in service to one's community.

Inspired by Gennep, mythologist Joseph Campbell spoke of Departure, Initiation, and Return, as well as the expanded phases below. This is the story arc of the Hero's Journey often told in classic movie scripts, such as *Star Wars* and *Lord of the Rings*. This is the journey any adult facing crisis may leverage to get to the gold of his or her life.

For a deep dive into Campbell's articulation of initiation, check out his classic book, *The Hero with a Thousand Faces*. Below is a synopsis. Consider where you are on the journey.

SEPARATION / DEPARTURE
Movement away from old world

Ordinary World • Call to Adventure • Refusal of the Call • Meeting the Mentor • Crossing the Threshold

LIMINALITY / INITIATION
Entering the dark forest, the ordeal

Test, Allies, Enemies • Approach to the Inmost Cave • The Ordeal • Reward

INCORPORATION / RETURN
Bringing the gifts home to others

The Road Back • The Resurrection • Return with Elixir

The Initiatory Journey

I use the phrase Initiatory Journey instead of Initiation because I believe it is more congruent with how initiation happens today. We don't just go on a hillside for four days and nights without food and water and magically come down as initiated adults. I went through five vision quests over seventeen years trying to find that "magic pill" of initiation. While the quests were enormously impactful, in the end, it was the integration of those fasts with everyday life itself—the day in and day out of coping with my wife's illness, of raising my son, of holding a business together—that was the true catalyst for my initiation. The challenges of intimacy, sex, and love in marriage were my teachers.

The tribulations of accountability, depletion, and boundaries at work helped me mature. The confrontation of my own core wounds and childhood demons enabled my growth as a parent and a person.

The battles of ordinary life are the guts of initiation today in the modern world. The setting may involve an eighteen-year marriage, a three-year job stint, or a seven-year parenting cycle. The forces of initiation build up over days, weeks, months, and years. And then one day—BOOM!—they erupt. A job loss. An affair. A divorce filing. A heart attack. A death. Logic gets flipped on its head, and in an instant, one's world is never the same.

Steeped in its own wisdom, the Initiatory Journey is a form of course correction. It happens when we have lost our way, when the forces of "What am I doing all this for?" surface from down under. These are the Grand Opportunities of Life. How can we leverage them?

To Suffer with Meaning

"Before the truth 'sets you free,' it tends to make you miserable."

– Richard Rohr, *Falling Upward*

I love the quote above for its raw honesty. As a culture, we only emphasize the upbeat "set you free" part. We don't have much tolerance or stamina for misery. In fact, we'd prefer to take a pill, suppress the pain, and get on with it. Most people, if given the choice, would opt to never hit a crisis in life. I get it. Who wants to suffer? But as the Buddha reminds us, life brings inevitable suffering. The question for each of us is not whether or not we experience suffering, but what do we do with it? Do we make meaning of it or not?

In the Pulitzer Prize-winning novel *The Sympathizer* by Viet Thanh Nguyen, the Vietnamese main character, an astute observer of American life, speaks of America and its "Disneyland ideology"—a culture in which we view "unhappiness as a moral failure." Is it not true that we judge ourselves as a failure if we experience unhappiness? Only in Disneyland, do we think we can get through life without experiencing unhappiness.

We all take knocks. It's inevitable. The optional part is what we do with it. As author and Jungian analyst Robert A. Johnson says in his book *Owning Your Own Shadow*, "One can endure any suffering if it has meaning; but meaninglessness is unbearable." Suffering presents a way to get to the golden vitality of life—new freedoms, bold loves, open possibilities, fearless emancipation. If we choose to, we may embrace the uprising, embrace the new life that awaits us, and produce meaning from suffering. Johnson goes on to say, "to suffer one's confusion is the first step in healing."

Refusing the Call: Spiritual Bypass

That night, all those years ago, I sat on the dream bed in the dream house, totally confused. I had no idea that I was being called to an initiation. Yet something mysterious tugged at me, challenging me to move away from my marriage and be willing to lose everything as I knew it. But I was frozen. Clearly, my life had turned into a nightmare; still, I was incapable of making changes. The initiatory journey confronted me in ways that I feared. I was scared of betraying my wife, being a bad man and "not on her team"—but it was becoming impossible to deny that things needed to change. For years, I refused the call for change, the call to adventure as Campbell called it. I danced with it, knew it was in the room with me, and engaged it in a way that barely kept my head above water.

Many people refuse the call by numbing themselves with alcohol, pot, pornography, or work. In my case, I had spent years leaning into my pain, like a boxer seeking redemption with each blow absorbed. For me, the numbing came in the form of masochism, a dancing in chains, a leaning into my own suffering, a martyrdom. Look at me, I'm meeting it all head on to be a better man—when in truth I was in denial of my emotional reality. I was miserable and suffering to the point of exhaustion and a nervous breakdown.

In the heart of darkness, I ran hard to be strong for my family— working, cooking, cleaning, balancing most of the logistics for our son. When time permitted, late at night or early in the morning, I secluded myself to my man cave in our basement, a psychological-spiritual isolation chamber where I had set up a private space and altar. A spiritual man on a spiritual mission, I journaled, processed, did shadow work, self-coached, and read Rumi, Hafiz, and Kabir, determined to make meaning out of my suffering. I engaged my misery, safe in the process and unwilling to act. *If I am strong enough, spiritual enough, soulful enough, I will get through this and be bigger afterward,* I told myself. *I will honor my family, my wife will get well, and we will live happily ever after, stronger in the end for it all.* It seemed noble and in line with my heroic male programming. Rescue the damsel in distress. Be strong for your family. Be a man. In truth, I was a naïve male trying to be a superhero.

Spiritual athleticism, poet Robert Bly called it in the poetry anthology *The Rag and Bone Shop of the Heart.* Trying to be at the mountaintop when you're at the base. A denial of reality. My approach was narcissistic and self-destructive. Since I did not have the courage to speak the truth of my emotions, I co-opted my wife's illness for the only gain I could still imagine: my own personal growth. She became a project through which I could heal my core wounds. In my spiritual practice, I sought to transform resentment into gratitude. I tried to make light from shadow, jewels from hardship. And while I felt the light and grappled with my shadow, the jewels did not materialize. I had forgotten the most important step—to listen to my soul.

In fear of failing my family, I ignored what my soul wanted of me—to leave my wife. To avoid this hard truth, I used spirituality to bypass anger and fear. I became a spiritually strong wimp, a wife-hater, and a momma's boy, needy for my wife's love and touch. I was deep in the mother wound, transferring the mother-pleasing behavior of my youth to my wife. Don't upset momma became synonymous with don't upset your wife. I was unconscious, uninitiated, and lacking mentors and guides. No wonder it got so bad before I answered my soul's call.

Chapter 3

Taking the Leap to Colombia

"Afraid that our inner light will be extinguished or our inner darkness
exposed, we hide our true identities from each other.
In the process, we become separated from our own souls.
We end up living divided lives, so far removed from
the truth we hold within that we cannot know the
'integrity that comes from being what you are.'"

– Parker Palmer, *A Hidden Wholeness*

For years, I perceived my inner light as that which I brought to others, specifically to Marisa. How I loved her, gave to her, and helped her get well. If I betrayed this narrative, I feared my light's extinguishment. I feared my inner darkness would be exposed. My weakness, inability to cope, and the ultimate taboo—my wanting to leave her.

And yet, when I stopped resisting what my soul was asking of me, my fears diminished. I came to realize that I had already lost so much. I began to understand that my light lived within me. It was the *source* of my gifts for others and not dependent on others. My light was dimming by staying in my marriage as it was. I had been separated from my soul for far too long, giving when I desperately needed to receive. It was only when I acted on the call to change that I began to experience "the integrity that comes from being what you are."

California and Amtrak

The summer trip to California was on. My wife and son were on their way to L.A. via Amtrak. I had dropped them off at the train station that morning in Denver. Marisa was "returning home," as she would say about the Pacific Ocean.

I didn't doubt that she suffered living in land-locked Colorado—the mile-high altitude, the extreme temperature swings, the dryness. I saw how alive and happy she became by the ocean. She began to talk of a permanent move to the West Coast. *Maybe her health might actually improve living there*, I thought. Maybe not, since vacation was different than daily living. Regardless, I was unwilling to leave our business, our son's school, and the Rocky Mountains for the traffic, smog, and crowds of Los Angeles.

And then there was Amtrak. My wife enjoyed "the process of the journey" on the train. The sense of "getting there." The down time— no Wi-Fi, limited cell service, nothing to do, no place to go. I had taken Amtrak once before. "I'm not doing that again," I said, drawing a rare boundary. To pay triple the cost of flying for lousy service, behind schedules, and twenty hours of travel? Forget about it. I was flying and would meet them there.

It was evening when I got the call. Marisa was hysterical in tears. Her sinuses were acting up. Her head was exploding going over the pass of the Rockies. She felt horrible. They had to stop the train. A paramedic had come aboard. She'd likely have to get off, she said.

I held my tongue and breathed deeply as she went on about her challenges. I wanted to say, "Wasn't the train supposed to be easier on your sinuses than the plane? Why did we pay triple the price?" Whatever. I wasn't going there. I felt what I had felt often in recent years: helpless, trapped, and angry. This drama again? Over the years, there had been many. I was done. Twenty-four years of empathic distress had dried me up. Kaput. Gone. I was no longer willing to bypass my emotions. Despite all of this, the old inner critic still screamed, *What an inconsiderate asshole you are!*

Fear of Expulsion

> *"Evolution has programmed us to feel rejection in our guts. This is how the tribe enforced obedience, by wielding the threat of expulsion."*
>
> – Steven Pressfield, *The War of Art*

Over the last decade, rejection had regularly punched me in the gut with those eight words: "I don't feel like you're on my team." In one phrase, Marisa could leverage the fear of expulsion living deep in the marrow of my bones. Whether done consciously or not, she knew how to enforce my obedience. The fear of losing connection drove me to dishonor myself.

When we are not enough for ourselves, we fear not being enough for others. We fear change in our most precious relationships. We fear expulsion from our tribe of two. It is primal and unconscious. The fear is that if we honor ourselves and speak our truths, we will lose the one we love. This keeps us in the dependency of a child instead of the sovereignty of an adult.

We say to ourselves: I can't tell him that I feel invisible; he'll hate me for it. I've tried to tell her how I need more touch; she's just not open to hearing it. The fear of expulsion is first experienced as a child when we fear losing a parent's love. You were bad! Go to your room! These serve as a primal shock to a child's nervous systems. From this moment on, many of us spend the rest of our lives doing everything we can to avoid rejection, to please the ones we love. Others avoid expulsion by becoming the ones who threaten it.

Either way, we must confront our primal fear or we become prisoner to it. The fear of losing love is the primary reason people stay in relationships that no longer serve them—for years, decades, and even for life. But is it really love? A nourishing love that makes you bigger in spirit, heart, and soul? Or a status quo love, hedged in security, that keeps you small and in fear?

> *"When we don't listen to our intuition, we abandon our souls.*
> *And we abandon our souls because we are afraid*
> *if we don't, others will abandon us."*

> – Terry Tempest Williams, *When Women Were Birds*

Unconsciously, we make a deal: If I betray my own well-being, you can't. I was no longer willing to make such a deal and abandon myself. Free of fear, I let go of trying to be on my wife's team. There was no team. It was me betraying myself to pretend. What about my team? She didn't seem to recognize the team that I needed. Until that moment, neither had I. Something, however, was shifting. The threat of expulsion no longer elicited my obedience.

Self-Betrayal No More

As Marisa spoke hysterically of the paramedic, the sinuses, I said, "Uh huh. Yep. I hear you," eking out a facade of empathy. I breathed into the nuance of guilt I felt without falling to it. I sat with what I knew. I was angry. I was done.

It was me, I knew. The anger was my emotional reality, not hers. *She* was not doing this to me. *I* was doing this to myself. I enabled it. It was time for me to take responsibility for what I felt. I did not try to brush it aside for fear of what would happen to our relationship. I had done that too many times before. I knew the cost. Instead, I trusted what I knew and felt my fears.

I was clear on what I'd been already mulling over for days, what I had to say. All my arguments with myself were exhausted. The burdens of her health would not diminish once she got off the train. I had no interest in pretending to vacation in Southern California; this would be no vacation. The driving forces of my life were changing. The skeletons were coming out of the closet. It was time to leap.

When Your World Erupts

At the pinnacle of self-betrayal, suffering reaches a breaking point. The cost of keeping love, be it silence or pleasing our partner, outweighs the benefit of keeping it. Love at this point is not healthy love. It's a meekness, negotiated comfort, and false security of habit. A love that no longer enhances our life force but depletes it. A love that makes our lives smaller, not bigger. A love that dims our spark as a couple.

At the threshold of the leap, our primal concern is recovering our life force. We advocate for the raw material of our well-being. We can no longer accept relational mediocrity with saying, "Everything can't be great all the time," when we really mean, "I want more from my relationship." We reattach to our soul. It supersedes the fear of expulsion from the tribe. Often, we must hit rock bottom in order to arrive here.

So, how do you know you've hit your edge, the threshold I'm describing? The moment when you're ready to emancipate? You know when you hear a voice that says, *I'm done, I can't do this anymore.* Eventually, it grows so loud that whatever needs to die—your relationship, job, or an old way of being—becomes so hard to continue that it feels like death. It's as if you're going mad or falling apart. At the extreme, your physical health may even fail.

In addition to my marital struggles, I was suffering at work. I had been at the same job for fourteen years in the company I co-owned with my wife. Bored to death, answering sixty perfunctory administrative emails per day, I struggled to show up day in and day out. Often, it felt like lifting a 250-pound weight over my head and walking around like that all day. Every few months, I imagined soaking the piles of paperwork on my desk with lighter fluid and torching them. I always used to joke that the hardest job to quit was the one in the company I owned. And yet I stayed because we made a good living and I feared the unknown. How could I quit the company I co-owned with my wife? How would I make a living? How could I pull the rug out from under us? Our entire lives were built on me showing up—our home, our livelihood, our family, everything. And yet the work felt dead to me, uninspired. I had no heart in it.

A Divided Life No More

"I had actively participated in every moment of the creation of this life—so why did I feel like none of it resembled me?"

– Elizabeth Gilbert, *Eat Pray Love*

In her best-selling memoir that became a popular movie, Elizabeth Gilbert speaks to the threshold. Her old life is unwinding. She has hit that moment when she knows things must change.

"It was a cold November, around three o'clock in the morning. My husband was sleeping in our bed. I was hiding in the bathroom for something like the forty-seventh consecutive night, and—just as during all those nights before—I was sobbing. Sobbing so hard, in fact, that a Great Lake of tears and snot was spreading before me on the bathroom tiles, a veritable Lake Inferior (if you will) of all my shame and fear and confusion and grief.

I don't want to be married anymore.

I was trying hard not to know this, but the truth kept insisting itself to me.

I don't want to be married anymore. I don't want to live in this big house. I don't want to have a baby."

Like a siren to that won't stop wailing, the words keep coming to Gilbert: *"I don't want to be married anymore."* She's not merely "ambivalent" about her marriage, but "utterly consumed with dread" at the idea of staying in it. The truth is crushing her. She chronicles all that she has set herself up for, and wonders, "How could I turn back now?" And yet how could she not?

"The only thing more unthinkable than leaving was staying; the only thing more impossible than staying was leaving. I didn't want to destroy anything or anybody. I just wanted to slip quietly out the back door, without causing any fuss or consequences, and then not stop running until I reached Greenland."

Gilbert knows something must change, but has yet to trust it. She can't just put on the mask of New York socialite or aspiring mommy anymore. Her inner world is exploding and her soul is rebelling. She feels crazy and sick. The cost of silence with her husband is more than she can stand. She can't "behave" anymore just to keep appearances. But change terrifies her—especially the hurt she may cause her husband. The benefits of change are unclear from the cliff's edge. Regardless, she can no longer live a divided life, separated from her soul.

At the Threshold

Whatever our truth is—be it "I'm done" or "I don't want to be married anymore"—if we are there, we are at the threshold. It may have taken months, years, or even decades to get there. Either way, there is no meaningful path but to make a change. And this is a scary moment, when old compressed life forces erupt from within a closed chamber. It is here that we could be dangerous.

Every day, people recklessly blow up marriages, commit adultery, and go savage with lawyers during a divorce, ignoring their children's best interests. Lives get fractured. An earthquake severs the landscape. We fragment, fall apart, and often self-destruct, creating more harm to the ones we love.

It is at this moment that I see many of my clients. They come to me in crisis, exhausted, barely making it through their day. They've had it. They're done with their old ways and they're scared. Good people who wonder: What do I do? How can I figure this out? How can I act with kindness to my partner while speaking this difficult truth?

In this moment, we rarely have an answer. We are immobilized with fear and paralyzed with uncertainty. Deep in the unravelling of knowledge, disorientation takes hold. Where am I? How did I get here? Action feels like an abstraction.

Soul Alignment – A Healthy No to A Healthy Yes

As Marisa spoke into the phone, I felt clearer than ever. She was no longer my primary concern. *I* was. Reconnecting to my soul, my body felt different, lighter, more joyful. It was a stark contrast from the powerlessness I had felt for many years. Something was happening to me. Embodied, lucid, I spoke what I had feared saying for years, what I had been thinking for months prior to that moment.

I held the phone tightly in my sweaty palm. I did not fear the sky falling. It had fallen before and I had survived. And then, I said the words.

"I'm not coming to L.A."

I paused, waiting for a reply. There was none. Only silence. I could only imagine the shock, disbelief, betrayal, and abandonment she was feeling. And then I stepped in further.

"I'm going to Colombia," I said.

I could no longer abandon my needs or forsake my dreams for hers. I considered my son's feelings, but I knew he couldn't understand the depth of these things.

Determined to honor myself, Colombia was my metaphor for freedom. It was a dream that had been tugging at me for decades that I had foresworn. How could I leave her? How selfish. She couldn't travel to a third world country. Use *our* money for *my* trip? That was wrong. And yet, we had been using our money for years to go to California.

Colombia was international travel in the Spanish-speaking Americas. Colombia connected to a deep part of me that sought risk, passion, freedom, and a chance to use my Spanish again, twenty-two years after learning it in Seville, Spain. It brought me to a dream that I'd had prior to getting into a relationship at age twenty-two, a dream of travelling to far away and exotic places. But now I'd be an older, wiser, international traveler. It was a dream that my wife could never be a part of because of her health—or, at least, her perception of it.

I gushed at the prospect of dreaming again, of living life on my own terms. I longed to travel alone, to connect with a good friend from Denver, a Colombian native, and meet his family for the first time. He would be visiting them in Bucaramanga, known in Colombia as "la ciudad de los parques." I could see firsthand the legendary land of the dangerous, drug cartel, which was no more. I would go to Bogota, Cartagena, Santa Marta, and a slew of rural villages in the Andes for three weeks. I had already booked the ticket the day before without communicating to my wife; I had never done that before.

The moment when I made the decision and spoke those shocking words to her, something came alive in me—a life force, a vitality, a freedom—that has not left me since, even in the face of my son's resentment and great familial hardship. I reconnected to the adventure of my life, which had been put on hold for years. It was an emancipation into a life where, after much personal work, I became the person I always sought to be—a man of passion, honesty, transparency, integrity, love, strength, and actualized ambition.

During the next few years, I continued my travels to Mexico City, Guanajuato, Chiapas, and Yelapa, as well to Spain multiple times—Madrid, Granada, the Alpujarras Villages, Barcelona, Costa Brava, Santiago De Compostela, and Galicia.

The travels, while real and phenomenal, became metaphors for the adventure of my daily life. The separation from the mundane prison I had been living in. I was challenging the forces of fear and self-betrayal within me while cultivating fearlessness, which was not the absence of fear, but the presence of courage in its face. All of this was a precursor for the biggest adventure of my life still to come, a reinvention of who I was and how I lived.

Abdication

Before the Colombia moment, I had been living in abdication. At its most basic definition, abdication means checking out. I had given everything over to my wife, and was abdicating the part of myself that refused to take responsibility for my own happiness. I was living like a dependent child instead of a sovereign adult, expecting others to be for me who I was not for myself.

I abdicated to be on my wife's team and keep a home together for my son. It was a deep imperative within, a redo of my own childhood—to give my son the loving presence of a father that I did not have at his age. To be clear, my wife, son, and I had many enjoyable moments over the years—the wholeness, love, and play of family. We were and still are kind and loving people who can enjoy one another. But, as I've said, I felt great incongruence within me. This caused suffering that had lost all meaning. And this is the end result of abdication.

When we abdicate, we avoid a part of ourselves and check out from what's in front of us. We get stuck in a cycle of looking away or blaming. Abdication is epidemic in our culture today, expressed in road rage, vitriolic talk news, and fear-baiting politicians. The list goes on— outer projections of an inner dynamic. We flip off other drivers to release personal anxiety. We strike out verbally at others when lacking an authentic voice. Unconsciously, we try to get safe by acting out, exploding on the ones we love when we're overwhelmed. It's a form of armor which locks us out of our own hearts and protects us from the hurt we might otherwise feel within. We do it to get safe—falsely safe.

Waking up to the costs of abdication is hard work. It requires stepping in and challenging the status quo. It's scary and might upend your life. You might not go to work tomorrow. You might upset the people you love. You might step away from your family or decide to alter the structure of your primary relationship. All cards are on the table. And what an exciting place to be!

Abdicators and Usurpers

In *The King Within*, Jungian psychoanalyst Robert Moore and theologian Douglas Gillette write about the dynamics of abdication. While their target audience is men, the passage applies equally to women:

> "The abdication syndrome results when a man projects the archetypal King [his power] onto someone else rather than integrating the energy into himself. It is interesting that every abdicated king needs at least one usurping king and every usurper must find willing abdicators."

The authors speak to how we give away our power and authority to someone else—a loved one, a parent, a boss—instead of stepping into it ourselves. That someone else is the usurper, the one willing to take the authority we abdicate from. We rely on the usurper in order to abdicate. We project onto others what we fear in ourselves.

It's his fault.
She made me do it.
My boss sucks.

Through blame, we avoid taking responsibility for getting our own needs met. We give away our power and authority to another rather than owning it ourselves. We abstain from taking a hard look at our weaknesses, strengths, and fears. In a phrase, we reject healthy adulthood and self-relationship. But once we reverse this pattern, we wake up to a wealth of energy and possibility.

Killing the L.A. Dream

I came back from Colombia a month later happy and energized, having had the adventure of a lifetime. I'd ventured into remote parts of the country, speaking Spanish daily and making friends and meeting people from all over the world. I'd hiked from the cobblestone streets of Barichara, a little village in the center of the country, to a friend's rural retreat center where I'd tasted the local delicacy of hormigas (fat ants). I'd walked the mountainous Caribbean Coast of Tayrona National Park and ridden horseback through the jungle. I'd toured a finca, a coffee plantation high in the northern mountains that has the most dramatic elevation gain in the world, from sea level to over 18,000 feet in less than 20 miles—creating some of the world's most treacherous sailing conditions off the coast. I'd experienced the massive wealth inequity of Bogota, with its Miami-luxury high-rise condos within a half mile of slums. I'd experienced things I had never thought possible as a man resigned to the supporting role of a major lifetime domestic production.

Coming home to Boulder, I wanted to try to make my marriage work again. Maybe with travel, advocating for what I needed, I could be happy. I did not have to put my wife's needs before my own always, but only when I felt it absolutely necessary. I could take responsibility for what I needed. Upon my return, my wife and I reconciled and experienced mutual affection and renewed appreciation for one another.

I even agreed to go L.A. on a two-month sabbatical to give California "a real try." Maybe L.A. was the answer after all. We just needed to do it for real. And so, we took a two-month house rental in Atwater Village, an artistic hamlet on the east side of L.A. My son did online schooling for a quarter. We managed our business remotely. I enjoyed my time there, accessing culture, arts, and diversity sorely lacking in Boulder. I often hiked in the San Gabriel Mountains only twenty minutes from my door. It was a great break from regular life.

Within several days of returning to Boulder from L.A., the joy ride came to a halt. Pushing us to make a real move to L.A., my wife had had us touring houses. Still on the house search back in Boulder, she came into our bedroom with her laptop to show me her "L.A. dream home."

I looked at it, shocked.

"Do you realize it's double the mortgage and half the square footage of this house?"

"We can make it work. I'm sure of it."

"Sorry, this is madness. Leaving the business, Jake's school."

"You can't do this to me! You're killing my dream!" She threw up her hands and stormed out of the room.

My jaw dropped. "*My* dream." The words pierced me. I was stunned. *My* dream. *My* team. I felt invisible. There was no "our dream." Had there ever been?

Several days later, I moved out.

Chapter 4

Conscious Emancipation: Assessing the Leap

"To draw the skeletons out of the closet is relatively easy, but to own the gold in the shadow is terrifying."

– Robert A. Johnson, *Owning Your Own Shadow*

I'm done, was all I could think. I stayed with friends—sleeping on couches, in spare bedrooms, wherever I could. All that mattered was having space from Marisa. The skeletons were out of the closet. How would I own the gold? This was the moment I'd been waiting for my entire life. I was primed for it. I had married into it with no idea it was coming many years down the road. Like so many of my clients, I had stumbled toward it, unaware it was the opportunity of a lifetime. Unfortunately, our mainstream culture has no framework for embracing this opening. The derogatory "midlife crisis" doesn't cut it. And this is why many of us reach this moment feeling like we've been hit by a semi-truck. With education, we can recognize these times for what they are—a call to awaken.

Why We Self-Betray

While there are many versions, we self-betray for two primary reasons: to maintain love and to stay safe. Below are variations of each. The voices we often hear are in italics.

To Maintain Love...

- We don't speak our truths - *I can't ask that of him.*
- We avoid conflict - *She'll get upset if I do that.*
- We falsely benefit our partner - *He needs me to love him just as he is.*
- We stay small - *At least he loves me.*

To Stay Safe...

- We do what's easy - *Whatever she says is fine with me.*
- We don't take responsibility for ourselves - *He told me to do it.*
- We refuse change - *I can't even consider life apart from her.*
- We avoid getting big - *I could never do that.*

Do any of these speak to you? Maybe you don't say what you need from your partner. Maybe you avoid change of any form when it's uncomfortable. However you may abdicate, you have an opportunity to emancipate. Often, we won't leap until the costs are no longer bearable. The question is, can we leap in a way that confronts our fear of loss, honors the one we love, and respects the gifts we've created?

How Would I Land?

I had made the leap. The skeletons were out of the closet and the gold was rising. Energy flowed back into me. It was as if a giant thumb that had been pressing down on me for years had suddenly been removed. The voice saying, *Be a good man, don't you dare betray her,* no longer held me back. I felt the sun rising in all parts of my being, seeing in a way that I had not seen before. It was an infusion of fresh air and perspective. For the first time in over a decade, I had full license to care for and be with just myself.

Over the years, I had given my all to our marriage. When sexual intimacy was scarce, I saw a sex therapist. As it turns out, I was not a sex addict. When we ran into the same old roadblocks of my not being on her team, I pleaded with my wife to go to couples therapy. We went for a short while, until she said it was too much for her health. When I needed to work on myself, I saw a coach. For now, there was no more work to be done on us. I was free.

How would I land after the dust settled? How would I reconfigure myself? I had no idea. And yet I was flying, the wind in my hair, exhilarated with the open road ahead. I was free from the twenty-year entanglement of my marriage. I trusted that if I could make it to this point, I would figure out the rest. With help, I learned to emancipate consciously.

Conscious Emancipation

Conscious emancipation. What is it? Why bother? Conscious emancipation liberates us from self-betrayal into self-honoring— honoring ourselves to love and be loved authentically, to find purpose, be fearless, and meet life head on. It enables us to engage the changing forces of our lives, to listen to what our souls are asking of us. As Robert Johnson says, "the skeletons" are coming out of the closet. The benefits of the old ways are exhausted. The cliffside beckons for big life changes.

In conscious emancipation, you are a pioneer on a fresh trail, travelling where nobody has gone before—to a you who has never existed. The invitation here is to blaze the trail to the unique you that the world has yet to know, an unknown you who is still developing. Others may have taken a similar path, but no one has travelled yours.

As I emancipated, my path was symbolized by a recurring archetypal dream in which I was a giant creature with a massive wingspan— a kind of pterodactyl soaring above a pre-historic landscape. For years, I had been caged in a tight canyon, a giant bird flapping its wings angrily, frustrated but never getting full extension past the stone walls. Shortly after I left my comfort zone (literally, my home in Boulder), the dream transformed into one in which I leapt out of the canyon and emerged to soar into an ancient Edenic valley of lush green grasslands, tall trees, opal lakes, and rivers, full of animal and plant life. In the dream, I realized I was flying, yet was uncertain of my wings, overwhelmed at the vastness of the landscape and fearful of tumbling to the earth. Eventually, I relaxed, trusted my wings, and flew, guided by an inner sense—somehow, I already knew how to fly. I held on to this archetypal image as a clear sign that I was on the right path.

Freedom of the air was mine. I reflected and prayed on it, inspired to keep stepping into the new flight that beckoned me forward. This meant playing on a bigger playing field, taking more risks in my work, stepping into larger roles, delicately navigating my marriage, and taking on the dream of writing this book.

Conscious emancipation is not about recklessly blowing up your life. Certainly, in tough moments, we may need to take decisive action—file divorce papers, quit a job, or leave a relationship—but we do it with agency, sovereignty, and love. Too many people swing a hatchet carelessly when they could do better for themselves and their loved ones. In the thick of crisis, we must pause and survey the landscape around us, not just react.

In this moment, cognitive dissonance often shows up as a guide—albeit a confusing one—telling us we're damned if we do and damned if we don't. "Should I stay or should I go now? If I go there will be trouble. If I stay it will be double," sang Joe Strummer of The Clash. It seems that either way we're screwed. But conscious emancipation may help us.

Conscious emancipation dissolves cognitive dissonance. You may take the leap *and* also honor the ones you love. You can speak your truth lovingly *and* move away from what no longer serves you. You can feel the hurt of those impacted by your actions *and* still act. You may step into the gauntlet and own it. It will hurt like hell at times, and you may fear falling apart, but the view is different. You see the opportunity and meet your fear with courage. You don't just destructively project it onto others. You grow through it.

Make Friends with Fear and the Loss of Who You've Become

"To become truly fearless, we must stop running from our fear and begin to make friends with it. We must learn to smile at fear."

– Chögyam Trungpa, *Smile at Fear*

To smile at fear is to reframe it, to see it as an ally and a friend and extract its message. When smiling at fear, we may even say, "Thank you, fear, for your teachings." In my experience, fear is often a protector, warning us about the dangers of blowing up our lives. If we listen to our fear, it may guide us to reconfigure our lives with prudence. In mining our fears, we may pull out many beautiful rubies. Fear has much to teach us about our weaknesses. To make friends with fear is to show up in life fully. This is the antidote to abdication.

When a version of a relationship seems to be done, fear grabs us on the most primal level. However, when we listen deeply, we understand this is really about the death of an old self. Psychotherapist and author Esther Perel describes this in her book *Mating in Captivity*. "We go elsewhere because we are looking for another self. It isn't so much that we want to leave the person we are with as we want to leave the person we have become." While speaking explicitly about extramarital affairs, Perel's insight applies equally to anyone who has grown distant in a relationship.

The person you have become may be the one you are eager to leave, even more so than your partner. Before leaving your partner altogether, it would be wise to get clarity on this. You may ask yourself first, can I reinvent myself in my current relationship? Too many people leave one relationship to enter another and recreate the same old problems. *How did I end up here again?* they wonder. Well, you never dealt with who you were in your initial relationship. Doing the same thing over and over again expecting different results is the definition of insanity. And yet we do it all the time.

We repeat failed actions because in the fear of the unknown—Who will I be?—if we really look at ourselves, it's easier to project everything onto our partner. Instead, I encourage you to seize the opportunity to honestly ask yourself: How did I co-create this relational dynamic? Do I want to leave who I've become in my relationship or the relationship itself? This is a critical distinction and step in our maturation process.

In asking these questions, we can step into change wisely and responsibly. It's not all on our partner. He or she is not the cause of our challenges, but a catalyst for us to grow up and take responsibility for what we want. We are the protagonist. Fear is the messenger—be it the fear of losing your relationship or your old self. Cultivate a healthy relationship with fear, and you will come out stronger. Once you do, you will understand who and what you must leap into.

The Leap

There's no getting around it: taking the leap is daunting. If we've made friends with our fear, we recognize its presence as a good sign. We're on the cusp of something big. The leap comes in many forms—a divorce, separation, the end of a long-held job, moving to another state or country. All are big life changes. And yet, ultimately, the leap is defined by your perception of the distance from where you are jumping. We all have our own perceptions of what the leap is, based on our capacity for risk and change. If your partner has no idea you're unhappy, and you don't communicate, the leap to expressing your dissatisfaction can feel impossibly far. For the Wall Street broker who trades millions of dollars a day, telling his wife he wants more intimacy can feel like the biggest gamble of his life.

Every day at home and work, we leap into revealing or hiding who we are. Do we wear a mask or show up authentically? Are we honest? There are big leaps and small leaps daily. This is part of the regular rhythm of our lives. Just like weather patterns, we have natural cycles when it comes to change. Daily, weekly, and monthly, we contract, expand, or remain in status quo. Frequently, we fight the cycles, believing the contractions to be too painful and expansions too overwhelming. We become like a weathervane refusing to move with the wind. We'd rather be stiff and safe than move with the elements. But that's not how life works. We may think we can control our lives, but nobody dictates when change happens. Instead, we may choose how we engage with change. We can decide how to leap, whether it's six inches or a hundred miles.

When We Fear the Leap

What's the risk in leaping? Of leaving the old you? Of being in relationship in a new way? Do the benefits of staying safe and maintaining love in the old relationship outweigh the costs? Is it the kind of love that feeds you or depletes you? A love that expands your energy or one that contracts it? You may not know. You may just be starting to wake up. You may have to track it over time. Uncertainty can be terrifying.

Security is the mountain to which we cling. Nearby, the ledge of potential beckons. We check it out from every angle and back away, returning to the safety of the old self. *I can't jump if I still love her. I can't tell him I'm unhappy; he'll be upset.* Internal conflict can paralyze us. We are in a box that we cannot see beyond, and the larger landscape below is elusive. For some, it can take years. Others, months. Some jump, ready or not. Maybe you've been looking over the cliff of your marriage or job for a while now. You know you need a change, but insecurity wins out. You have the vision and insights, but you're still not moving forward. You're stuck at the edge, afraid of losing everything you've worked so hard for. Don't worry. This is a great place to be.

To Jump or Not?

Cynthia was forty-six years old with two boys, ages seven and nine. Over the years, she had been supermom, the main breadwinner who also ran the household with her husband Chris. They had been married for more than fifteen years. The last five had been an emotional desert. Chris rarely appreciated Cynthia, and affection was nonexistent. While Chris embraced his job as a full-time dad, he never wanted to be in the role.

When Cynthia came to see me, she said Chris still suffered from the shame of never having re-launched his career after an earth-shaking job loss years ago. As if trying to compensate for his loss of power as the main provider, he had emotionally shut off from his wife and given all his energy to the kids. She had tried to speak up about her needs—intimacy, affection, and sex—but he was uninterested, even apathetic. Furthermore, he raged on her about small things at least a few times per month, like the trash can lid not being closed properly or dishes left in the sink. She was baffled and felt like she was living with a stranger. He, on the other hand, thought everything was fine.

In my office, she pauses, feeling into the gravity of her thoughts. It is our fourth visit.

"What's going on?" I ask.

"I'm actually considering this."

"Considering what?"

"Not letting Chris run my life."

"And what's that look like?"

"I don't know." She breathes, tears in her eyes. "I can no longer be small with him."

I nod. She is in her truth.

"And I'm terrified of the consequences to my family."

She is considering leaving him.

"How you do you feel now?"

"Scared… and yet somehow calm."

Tears continue to swell in her eyes. She pauses, breathing slowly. I work with her so she may stay connected to her emotions and the wealth of information they offer her. She says she's not sure yet if she will stay or leave. She weighs the costs and benefits. We talk about a middle way, beyond stay or go. Maybe she can stay with a friend a few nights per week for the short term. Would Chris understand? Would he agree to it? She knows it's not his place to decide. Either way, she fears he will react explosively.

"He has no idea this is coming," she tells me.

Cynthia is on the cliff. She is rewriting an old script of being the peacemaker, which came from her family history as the oldest child in a family of four children. While she has felt invisible to Chris for years now, it has hit a breaking point in the last month. She suffers just being in his presence, like Elizabeth Gilbert in *Eat Pray Love*. Something in her says, *No more*.

The tears soften in her eyes. She doesn't want to answer if she will stay or go, and yet she knows she must.

"I need more time."

"For what?"

"To be with it all. I'm afraid I'll lose my boys. He's more connected to them than I am."

"I get it. But can you continue sacrificing yourself for them?"

She shakes her head. "No."

Living her life from the fear of loss is unsustainable. She knows this.

"But I want to stay in the house," she says. "I want to be close to them. I'm going to move out of our bedroom and into the basement."

And this is her leap for now.

From Confusion to Clarity

At the leap, I invite you to widen your lens. Look beyond the cliff into the larger landscape of what you are leaping into. Engage the fear of loss and do not confuse the fears with who they really are. Losing love or security can feel like death. And in many ways, it is. Be it the death of a tired relationship, an old you, or a life that no longer serves you. That feeling of dying inside is actually the voice of reason: *Something needs to die so that I may live.*

In conscious emancipation, we feel our primal fears but are not run by them. We engage fear so it doesn't escalate into terror. We understand that what we fear losing is often what we need to lose. To create a new relationship, we must let the old one die. To see anew, the old lens must be replaced. With a new view of relational restructuring, we need not fear losing the relationship itself. Instead of the daunting, *Who will I be without my family?* I invite a reframe to, *Who will I be in a new familial dynamic?* The reframe offers us opportunity rather than obstacle.

In my own experience, and with clients, I have seen that if we stay focused on the emancipation we seek and open to fear's teachings, clarity will arrive. We will know when and how to break with the old life. That voice inside of us may say: *I'm done, done with the old ways; I am so done; get me out of this old version of me and this relationship; something's got to change.* And then you're ready to jump, to leave the old life. This is exciting! Insight has become so strong that you know what you need to do. You're fearless!

A Concrete Target in Mind – What Are You Moving Toward?

Before you leap, first ask yourself if the leap is a move toward something or a mere escape from pain? Take a breath and look around. Get a clear view of the landscape. See what you're leaping toward. A new you? A new vision of relationship? Or perhaps a new life?

If we find that we are focused only on what we are escaping, the issue is that the energy of escape defines us. It is our only frame of reference. We live in a reaction instead of an affirmation. Our thinking revolves around the stress we seek to diminish instead of the light we wish to enter. And without clear direction, we may be left with regret after leaping wondering, *What did I do?*

At the same time, what we seek to escape from has gifts of its own to offer us. In it, there is critical information about what hasn't been working in our lives. Beware of feel-good New Ageisms that deny this, such as "stay positive" and "don't worry, be happy." Instead, integrate both what you seek to escape from *and* what you are leaping into. What we seek to escape from (what I call Enslavers) and what we may leap into (Emancipators) are yin and yang. One defines the other. In this way, we get to a wider path of wisdom beyond the chasm of hope and fear, to be at our most powerful.

Moving Away From and Toward

Jack stayed in his marriage for seventeen years, a model father and provider. He did it to get love and be validated by his wife, kids, and community. He did it to be okay by society's standards as a "normal" heterosexual male. The problem was, he was gay.

"I am not worthy to be who I really am," he says to me. "And…" he catches himself, "I don't believe that anymore."

"Yes," I say.

"If I try to be who I really am, I will lose my old life, my wife, my family, and my community, and… I can no longer pretend to be who I'm not for their benefit."

Jack considers the costs of coming out to his family. He can no longer bear the weight of wearing the mask of being straight. The inner combustion of living a lie has made him sick in his stomach over time. Something within his soul demands that he live with integrity in who he is. While clear on his direction forward, Jack's still a bundle of nerves.

I ask him to speak about what he is moving toward. He answers his real self, his true sexual orientation, his autonomy, freedom, and his ability to breathe freely again. The knowledge of his direction calms him down. A moment later, he speaks about what he is escaping—the untruth of his old identity, his old family system, and the people in his small town who are homophobic.

I look into his green eyes for a full minute or more, holding space for him and the immensity of his emancipation, seventeen years in the making. He relaxes. Being witnessed is healing for him.

"And is there anything in your old family system that you still value?"

"My relationship with my kids and my wife, of course."

"Yes. There are many gifts still there."

"For sure," he says.

While Jack's old way of being in his family cost him a lot, it also created many precious experiences and memories with his wife and kids. Love grew in all those years, even in the presence of his untruth. He knows that, and that's why he hid his sexual orientation for so long. But now, even though he fears losing his family's love, he knows he must chart a new path.

"Can you honor the love *and* be the new you who you seek to be?" I ask him.

He listens and pauses, fully present. I can see from the intensity of his gaze, a deep breath, and multiple mini-nods of his head that he believes he can do both. He appreciates how his old self benefitted him and how he must now be his true self. While confronting his fear of loss, he may also honor the gifts he created in his old family system. With consciousness of this, he need not reject all of who he was, but instead transform it into the healthier version of who he seeks to be.

Building Faith into Action

Once we see the gifts created from what we're moving away from, we can build greater faith with what we're moving toward. We can actually be grateful for the challenges we seek to escape from. This helps us stay real, not pretending happiness will just fall out of the sky. Instead, we trust the process and build faith in our movement forward. Faith and action are a chicken and egg deal. Faith grows as we move into action toward what we want in our lives. And action increases as faith grows.

Emancipators and Enslavers

A teacher of mine used to say, "What we resist persists." I'd like to add, "What we resist has the instructions to free us into what we seek." In the chart below, I've mapped out examples of the interplay of what I moved away from (Enslavers) and moved toward (Emancipators) in my relationship.

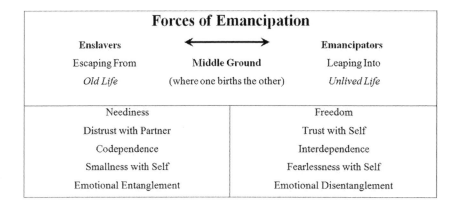

Forces of Emancipation		
Enslavers	⟵⟶	**Emancipators**
Escaping From	**Middle Ground**	Leaping Into
Old Life	(where one births the other)	*Unlived Life*
Neediness		Freedom
Distrust with Partner		Trust with Self
Codependence		Interdependence
Smallness with Self		Fearlessness with Self
Emotional Entanglement		Emotional Disentanglement

Unconscious Emancipation

Unconscious emancipation is the flip side of conscious emancipation. Sadly, it is the norm in our culture. It is a primal response to imprisonment and a life dominated by fear, as well as a lack of understanding of how to befriend fear. It often leaves a scorched trail of destruction and causes irreparable damage to our most valued relationships.

Every day, adults unconsciously emancipate themselves by yelling at partners, storming out of bedrooms, screaming at family, and slamming one another with divorce papers (or restraining orders, or other malicious litigation), handing over the powers that they could not manage themselves to bureaucratic institutions and lawyers who profit from conflict. I've seen this firsthand, and it is horrific—for the couple, the children, and the potential for a relationship to end consciously.

What if instead of divorce, we redefined the model to a third way, beyond stay or go? What if we called it Relational Transition, Conscious Uncoupling, or even Epiphany? What if we could cultivate an ally in our partner to alter our relationship? Or commit to deep courage and the willingness to be broken up, tutored and internally restructured by grief? Why don't we do this? Because we have little, if any, guidance on how to. Often, we have no understanding that it's even possible. And even with awareness and guidance, it is a path steeped in paradox.

Chapter 5

The Paradox of Leaping Wisely

"The intuitive mind is a sacred gift and the rational mind is a faithful servant. We have created a society that honors the servant and has forgotten the gift."

– Bob Samples, inspired by Albert Einstein

Paradox. It turns logic on its head. It is the domain of the intuitive mind and operates on a non-rational level. It is mind beyond mind. Through paradox, we may reconcile internal dichotomies and heal inner battles. We may cultivate mature adult parts of ourselves to live in self-trust, self-love, and sovereignty.

At first, paradox confuses us. It requires us to simultaneously hold two contradictory truths: "[Paradox] forces us beyond ourselves and destroys naïve and inadequate adaptations" (Robert A. Johnson, *Owning Your Own Shadow*). Often, what seems to make no sense makes perfect sense through the lens of paradox; it has a deeper wisdom to it. Paradox, I often say, is the language of the soul. A wise woman once said to me, "There is no confusion in life, only an inability to grasp paradox."

Paradox is paramount in conscious emancipation. The first paradox is this: Your obstacles are your gifts. Your dying marriage or restructuring relationship offers you a new beginning, new energy, new life, and perspective. Your soul-sucking job tutors you in what you need to leave behind and move toward. That which you seek to be free from has the instructions to free you. We get emancipated from obstacles when we begin to view them as opportunities offering us the exact instructions we need to get free. As a culture steeped in dualisms—good or bad, right or wrong, with us or against us—the idea that two contradictory voices can be true at the same time is revolutionary.

Tracking Paradox: Both/And

My paradox simply was "I'm done" and "I love her." The voices were contradictory and confusing, with many layers. The first said, I'm done trying to be on my wife's team. I'm done not being enough for myself, done putting aside my own needs and betraying myself. It was a most painful truth, one that I feared, as it conflicted so starkly with "I love her."

I remember tracking the voices, attempting to reconcile the two. They were in sharp contradiction to one another. The polarity was often overwhelming. I felt crazy, unstable, and confused. How could I leave her if I loved her? I swung on the pendulum from one voice to the other daily, weekly, monthly. The only way I could gain some sanity was by quantifying it. Some days it was 60% I'm done, 40% I love her. Other days, it was 30% done, 70% love her. Other days it was 10/90, 90/10. And over time, it levelled off to a consistent 90% I'm done and 10% I love her. And that was when I knew it was time to act, time to leap. The primal fear of losing her was superseded by the fear of losing myself.

Tracking was a way to resolve my madness and allowed me to hold both/and instead of just the either/or. It was a tactic to enter the deeper wisdom of paradox beyond the rational mind alone. I could go deep into what was ultimately true for me: seeing and honoring the "I love her" voice, even as I acted on the "I'm done" voice. From there, I gained the courage to do the hardest thing I've ever done in my life— to leave the woman I loved.

The Fine Thin Path of In-Between

"The wound is the place where the Light enters you."

– Rumi

Taking the leap looks different for everyone. Throw everything on the bus, get out of Dodge, and blow up your old life. Or back away from the cliff, stagnate, and do nothing. But there are many alternatives in between jumping explosively or not jumping at all. Often, the reward is much greater in this middle way—but it still has its risks and challenges.

In the audio series *The Wisdom of Joseph Campbell*, Joseph Campbell spoke of the pathless path. I often refer to it as the fine thin path, which is more concrete for my clients. This is the path of in-between, a narrow path—a fine line, to be exact—requiring acute attention, a samurai's seeing, and, yes, a master's guidance. This is the way of walking between that which you are moving away from and that which you are moving toward. The seeds of the new landscape blossom from what's been cultivated in the old lands. This is a way to move forward without destroying the gifts of all that you've created until now. For me, that was my family and my business. Most do not take the fine thin path, primarily because they do not know it exists or it seems too hard. As I've said before, we live in a culture of dualities not trained in, and often blind to, the subtle art of "in-between." The fine thin path offers a wider expanse of opportunities.

Keith - Stay or Leave

Keith has hit a threshold. His marriage has been compromised for a while. As hard as he tries, he cannot make his wife Sandra happy. He loves her greatly, but her disappointment in him distresses him. As we talk by video Skype, another truth emerges.

"She complains a lot about me," he says. "Like how I don't make enough money. I'm not around enough for our kids. I don't meet her needs. It's draining, to be honest."

"And? Is any of it true?"

"Some, but it's not the whole truth. I listen to her and I'm responsive. I've been looking at other work opportunities, and taking the kids to soccer lately."

"And what about her needs? How do you show up for her?"

"She hasn't been very specific about her needs. To be honest, she doesn't communicate all that much. And when she does, it's mostly complaints."

"And in the couples work you're doing? Does she communicate there?"

"She talks, but it's more like venting. The therapist says I need to validate her feelings."

"And do you?"

"I do. But I also feel like she's putting it all on me. Of course, I have my part."

He is quiet for a moment. He looks around, then up. I sense something else important and unspoken in his silence. A few moments later, he reveals that for several months now, he and Sandra have slept in separate bedrooms. Still, it's not enough, he says. He has proposed a temporary separation. But Sandra refuses to hear of it.

"'A real man does not leave his wife,' she says. 'A real man sticks through it all in marriage.'"

"Wow, that's a strong statement," I say.

He nods. "She can be harsh."

"You do know she's scared."

Keith nods again, visibly uncomfortable.

Over the next two weeks, Sandra digs her heels in. She threatens to divorce him if he leaves the house. Keith tries to explain that he still loves her. He just needs time to get perspective that couples therapy has not provided. He is seeking to redefine their relationship, not throw in the towel. But she will have none of it.

In a subsequent session, Keith looks at me, frustrated, a depleted look on his face. He is still at home. While he wants to move out, he fears losing his family. Sandra may vilify him to their kids. We work together so that he may stay strong with himself and compassionate with his wife. He feels the sting of Sandra's inflexibility, the opposite of the healthy love he seeks. The irony is that if Sandra were willing to meet him partway, perhaps suggest an alternative separation arrangement, she would be more likely to achieve the outcome she seeks of keeping their marriage together. She cannot see this. Keith is in a quagmire.

"Do you see the both/and here for you?" I ask him.

"What do you mean?"

"You want to honor *both* yourself *and* your wife."

"Yeah," he says.

"How do you do both? It's not easy, but from what I am hearing from you, it's the right way forward for you. Would you agree?"

"Yes."

In the weeks to come, Keith stays present with his fears of loss and his own growth. He navigates a fine thin path of honoring himself and his family. It's not easy, but he walks the way of in-between. While fear has its way with him at times, he engages his marital challenges to get bigger through it all. He learns to feel hard feelings, speak his needs to Sandra, and understand that whether he remains married or not, he can still honor his family. The path of in-between offers him and his family growth that they could not have attained otherwise.

My Fine Thin Path: Scalpel, not Hatchet

"The key to a good life is to be true to yourself and good to your people."

— Dene Maria Sebastiana, Life Coach

When I left my wife, I did not act on the fine thin path. Instead, a few days after the "you can't kill my L.A. dream house" episode, we sat in the office of a couples therapist we had seen before. I listened as my wife elaborated on how good things had become since our trip. I sat, stunned, as if we were living on different planets. When it was my turn, I spoke unambiguously.

"I need to move out."

This was the first I'd spoken of it. Fearful of her reaction, I remained calm. I needed space from my marriage; that was clear to me. I didn't see any other way. In five words, I had thrown down a stick of dynamite, seeking to blow a path through a mountain I couldn't see past. Once the debris fell back to earth, I would figure out what the new landscape offered me.

I had hoped the therapist would help me manage the fallout, but he did not—time was up. My wife was devastated. Outside the therapist's office afterwards, we sat in her car as she revved the engine in neutral. I pulled the keys out of the ignition until she calmed down. In the moment, I became aware of the delicate balance of compassion and caretaking. Over the next few months, with the assistance of my coach Dene, I did my best to follow the fine thin path.

"Scalpel, scalpel," Dene often said. "Not hatchet."

The scalpel enabled me to meet my fears of completely rupturing my relationship with my wife and son. It enabled me to honor them and make the changes I knew I needed to make. The scalpel, compared to the hatchet, was much slower, more delicate, and required more attention and intention. It was the fine thin path of in-between. It meant honoring my wife and son as well as moving forward as I needed to. It meant honoring continued connection *and* separation.

Over the next year, my wife and I did weekly check-ins and family dinners with our son. It became a sacred space that we could rely on, enabling connection *and* separation. We practiced courageous heartfelt communication in a pre-established container with strong agreements—a practice I strongly recommend for any couple experiencing distress in their relationship.

In hindsight, I can say the key with the scalpel is to own it and be patient with it, resisting the temptation to break out the hatchet. As much as I wanted to hack off my old life—a depleting marriage and an unfulfilling job—I paused and assessed the landscape at every turn with patience and perspective. Dene consistently encouraged me to be conscious of my choices. He had me look at my own projections and wounds triggers, all of which had to be fleshed out, so that I was not projecting onto my family. I could be true to myself and good to my family. Still, the path was often murky.

While I used the hatchet initially to get out of my house, over the next two plus years I used the scalpel in a very slow transition toward healing and relational redefinition. Our situation was even more fragile because we worked together; our entire family financial livelihood could easily be destroyed in one rash moment.

Furthermore, I knew the scalpel was the richest path possible emotionally and spiritually for me and the right path to love the family I still cared about. While I wanted to step into a new life that enlarged me, I did not want to destroy all the gifts I had cultivated up until that moment. The gifts included our long-shared history, a precious family dynamic, and a profitable business.

This was not easy in the face of forces pulling at me to break out the hatchet and flee to Spain or Mexico in any moment. Instead, I moved slowly and deliberately. I gave us time to acclimate to the new landscape. I hired out for most of my position at our business and risked a significant income cut. I stayed in Boulder and still travelled. I continued to separate from my wife and participate in our family. In the path of in-between, I worked hard to honor my desire for independence and autonomy as well as the presence my family still asked of me. Just because I used the scalpel, however, didn't mean there weren't any risks.

In any moment, Marisa could slam me with divorce papers, pursue litigation to restrict me from seeing my son, or abandon our business herself. The risks were real and daunting at times, but I worked at it daily, confronting my fears, trusting myself, and cultivating allies to support the vision of what I was moving toward. It was the vision of a bigger life without dependency on my wife for my well-being. It was about maintaining a modicum of trust where trust had been ruptured. And while my wife was devastated at first, through facing her own demons over the course of time, she became transcendent and emancipated as well. It was clear that we were done in this iteration of our relationship. Were we done for good? That was still to be determined.

Self-Care and Presence

When clients see me at the threshold seeking clarity, I immediately acknowledge the immensity of where they are. That place of big change, the cracking open of new life. They often do not see it. How could they? It is not in our cultural language. I emphasize the importance of taking it slowly, one step at a time. Not trying to figure out what's going to happen or how things will look in six months.

Too many individuals terrorize themselves with the unknown: Where will I live? How will I land? What will happen? This wreaks even further havoc on them, during such a fragile time of life change. Often their sleep bottoms out, they can barely function at work, and breathing may be hard. Instead of seeking certainty with elusive details, I coach my clients to be present with all that is happening. In this way, they may build trust with themselves. The difference during crisis between devastating pain and manageable suffering is presence.

With presence, you are with the enormity of the moment. You learn to conserve the precious energy you have when all the wind has been sucked out of you. You get done only what you have to, be it at work or at home. You do only what's essential and applaud yourself for showing up as you can. You set your sights on being half as productive as normal, or even less. Look at your task list and cross out what you don't have to do today, grateful that you are getting anything done at all. This is called self-care. It is critical. In a go-go culture, we don't know what self-care is. Instead, we seek to battle our way through everything. Our inner wisdom knows we'd be better served to put self-care at a premium during such times. In its absence, we crash and burn, often doing serious damage to our nervous systems and health in general.

Self-care enables presence, and presence enables one to fully meet crisis. This is where you have the opportunity to take massive leaps in your own growth. Where you can actually listen and understand what is happening to you. Why you ended up here. Change was needed. And big change is painful. Step in, knowing that you can only take one step at a time. And trust each step along the way, releasing the unknown of tomorrow, next week, or the months to follow. This is where you learn to come home to yourself. You stay in the moment and take it day by day—minute by minute, even.

Presence is a great gift to one at the precipice. It is how I got through my darkest hours—when losing my wife, family, and home felt like utter desolation, even though I had initiated it all. It is how time and again I have seen clients walk out of my office, lighter, more able to make it through their day and even with a smile on their faces.

Furthermore, when we're at the edge, we may create boundaries and agreements with our partner to honor one another, knowing this is hard on both of you. Give yourselves time and space apart, knowing you each must tend to yourselves like never before. On your own, sit quietly and breathe at least several times per day. Speak a simple affirmation to meet fear and breathe new life into your system.

In my most vulnerable hours in the terror of the deep night, a simple affirmation saved me when I was uncertain what I still had to live for, when the pain was so great that I was grateful I did not own a firearm. I feared all that I could lose, but knew I had to step forward. I said to myself, repeating over and over, fifty to a hundred times until I fell back asleep:

> "I love you.
> I know this is hard.
> We will get through this."

Self-Compassion: Sacred Fuck Ups

For years, I had fumbled along with a cursory blueprint of emancipation. I worked hard at it. Learning to value myself, independently of my wife; practicing self-regulation instead of just co-regulation; taking care of myself when I felt angry or sad; breathing when I was emotionally triggered. All of this was contrary to my typical M.O. of seeking her to make me okay. To reverse decades of programming required discipline and endurance.

Often, it felt impossible to get it right. I screwed up consistently. I'd project, fail to hold healthy boundaries, or speak before I knew my feelings. I called these "sacred fuck ups," a tongue-in-cheek term of compassion for hard-learned lessons. How could it be otherwise? I was reversing decades of old programming. Today, I appreciate my mistakes as great teachings to empower me. Every time we fumble, every time we fail, we may get back up and ask, "What is life trying to teach me? What is my partner trying to teach me? How can I love myself when I make mistakes?"

Allies

> *"Much of the work of midlife is learning to tell the difference between people who are still dealing with their issues through you and those who are really dealing with you as you really are."*

– Richard Rohr, *Falling Upward*

As we leap, it is critical that we get help from others who can see what we cannot see ourselves. A coach, therapist, friend, or elder who has looked over the cliff him or herself. Someone who can see opportunity and possibility at rock bottom. It's not just about having friends, but allies.

Allies, unlike friends, will lovingly reflect truth back to you without trying to fix you or make others wrong. Trusting the strength of their relationship with you, allies do not fear losing you. When we don't have such allies, there is a big hole in our self-care. In general, however, our culture doesn't understand the importance of true allies.

Many of us suffer far too long because we don't have a solid support system to encourage us. When we speak our truth, our family or friends often project their own biases on us with warnings like: "I told you he was worthless, I knew she was no good for you." Or, they might speak to us from their own fears. "You can't tell her that. She won't be able to hear you. How do you think she'll react?" Whether they're right or wrong, do they support you—at least, in your inquiry? Do they let you claim the right to ask hard questions? To be a sovereign adult? If not, they aren't the allies you need right now.

Finding allies is easier said than done. We live in a time where people are busier and less available than ever. Who can change a culture? I say you and I can. Why should we accept the small life that comes from going it alone without a tribe? Instead, I say we challenge current reality and manifest what we seek. I spent five years—yes, five years—patiently seeking out a strong group of allies in a men's group. Now, it's been more than fifteen years. My tribe is invaluable.

Find people who will sit with you in the hard questions, who will hold the inquiry with you and encourage you to stick with it. It could be friends, family, a support group, a coach, a mentor. It doesn't matter who, just as long as they are willing to be with you in the inquiry—without judgement, with presence, what Buddhists call bearing witness.

Mentors & Elders

Ideally, you get guidance from mentors and elders, those who have been down the path. In his work, Joseph Campbell speaks about how you can move through the hero's journey most efficiently with mentors, elders, and allies.

I could not have navigated my initiatory journey without my coach Dene, a fierce and wise advocate for me. He was a passionate individual from The Bronx, who spoke with a thick New York accent and held the wisdom of an elder. As my coach, I knew he was the right man for the job. I knew that investing in myself had to be my priority. The fulcrum within me had to be set right to lift me into the life that awaited me.

Another mentor and elder who was with me every step of the way was my dear friend Nick. He was a Dutch-American man with the wisdom of Old Europe in his bones. Passionate, but in a quiet calm way until you awakened the New Jersey in him. And beyond serendipitous—as a divorcee and divorce recovery coach, he knew well the terrain in which I was navigating. He was and is a great blessing in my life.

Mentors and elders are those who have been to hell and back and come out wiser and bigger because of it. They have successfully navigated their own initiatory journeys and returned with wisdom for others, what Joseph Campbell calls "returning with the elixir." And throughout the years, I was lucky to meet other such mentors and elders.

The Men's Leadership Alliance (MLA), in Boulder, CO, founded by Tom Daly, Keith Fairmont, and Jeffrey Duvall, arrived in my life at the age of thirty-three. While I had been doing the work of emancipation before I even knew it, I realized I needed community. I knew my needs could not be met solely at home. I looked around at my world, knowing something was wrong. I had no community, and no friends with whom I could share my deepest struggles. I knew that had to change—but how, I did not know. Then, I found MLA. Their retreats became my temple.

At those weekend gatherings, for first time I found men who could be fierce and tender, honest and vulnerable. For years, I attended their annual retreats, completing a wide variety of rituals and rites of passage processes. I once broke through a wall of twenty men representing my wife's West Nile Virus, the wall of illness that created such distance between us. Another time, I had a 250-pound man pin his knees on my arms as I lay on the floor on my back, just as my brother had done many times when we were kids.

Through re-enactments of traumatic situations, I could rewire them and free myself. I could not have done this work alone. I needed a strong container, held by individuals of character who knew what they were doing. I didn't need friends; I needed elders, mentors, and allies. Eventually, I was able to give back the gifts I had received. I staffed MLA events and then became senior staff, leading retreats with my dear friend and co-facilitator Jason Geoffrion, often with forty or more men.

In addition, I have been blessed to have many mentors and allies over the years. These are individuals I have loved, and who have loved me. They are people who held me accountable to be my best self, and I did the same for them. To find a tribe is no simple task. As I mentioned, it took me five years to find my first community of allies. I am grateful that I had the clarity to persevere in seeking the support I needed.

Our life is a blessing when we have a trustworthy community, one that welcomes our most challenged self with a commitment to our most vital and best self. Community is critical during a crisis, and is, in fact, often itself what our soul is calling for. We are wired for it, and that wiring is getting challenged like never before in an increasingly isolated and lonely culture. We cannot go it alone. The myth of the individual is just that: a fantasy. Alone, we will not thrive in this life or prosper through a crisis.

True to Self is Good to People

Conscious emancipation may begin as a self-centered journey, but it doesn't end there. Ultimately, we leap as an act of service for and beyond ourselves—for our expansion, integrity, vitality, and a healthy version of love, all of which are gifts to our family and the world. The gift of a more vitalized you brings freedom and also a higher responsibility.

"For to be free is not merely to cast off one's chains, but to live in a way that respects and enhances the freedom of others."

– Nelson Mandela

As Mandela says, freedom begins with removing our own chains. A bound man or woman is in no position to be an agent for change. To give love, we must dedicate ourselves to mastering love, trust, and respect within ourselves. Then, we may offer those gifts to others. Learn to be kind to yourself, and you can then be kind to others. Conscious emancipation offers us this opportunity. Otherwise, we may be operating from our woundedness, and the results of our love may do us and our partner more harm than good.

When you leap, being true to yourself may appear to be in opposition with being good to others. You may be accused of betrayal, or of causing your partner pain. This should be a red flag, indicating that your partner's making an excuse and projecting their own fear of what's gone wrong in the relationship onto you. Remember, when you are true to yourself, your partner benefits as well—but it requires that they engage their fears and step into the challenge with maturity.

You are saying, I am no longer happy with who I am in this version of us, I want to see if another way offers us new life or not. I am willing to take that risk, are you? In this moment, you are seeking a better version of yourself and your relationship. When you have integrity with yourself, there is no betraying others.

And yet when we fear hurting our partner, we are at a crossroads of identity. How do I become who I really want to be without hurting my partner? In conscious emancipation, we stay connected to who we seek to be. We don't fall into the mistake of judging ourselves for how we do or don't show up. We don't project that self-contempt onto others with emotional or physical violence. Instead, we own it with self-compassion, acknowledging the suffering that comes from being out of integrity with who we are. As we build our own self-compassion, we expand our capacity to experience compassion for our partner.

Conscious emancipation is taking action toward discovering self-love. We are flipping the switch from self-contempt to self-compassion. And while this primarily means being good to ourselves—listening to ourselves, eating right, moving slowly, doing less—we also need to maintain healthy boundaries with our partner, specifically if she or he comes at us with barbs. If attacks happen, we don't betray ourselves, thinking dishonestly that we deserve it or must ease others' pain. Instead, we stand compassionate and strong, loving ourselves and our partner from the place of witness. Often we need only to respond with something as simple as, "I feel your hurt" or "I'm sorry."

Still in the moment of hurt, our partner will often only see betrayal. I suggest you don't try to force feed him or her a truth that he or she is not ready to hear. Don't justify your actions with patronizing New Ageisms like *now you'll be set free too, dear*. Give your partner the space and time to mourn as needed. With every birth comes a painful death. This is true of all initiatory journeys. It certainly was true with mine.

When navigated skillfully, the hero's journey offers many gifts for ourselves and the ones we love. Through it, we come back stronger, bigger, and more powerful. But it is not an easy path, simultaneously a hell and paradise of sorts. As Joseph Campbell said in *The Hero with a Thousand Faces*, you must go through the dark forest and face the death of your old self in order to get to your new self and the gold of the life that awaits you.

Chapter 6

The Script and the Mask

"The deepest suffering is forgetting who we are."

– A Buddhist teaching,
Tara Brach from "Tara Brach" podcast

Conscious emancipation is a quest to remember who we are. We enter a new way of listening, knowing, and being with ourselves. Big life changes during the initiatory journey give us a lot of intense material— emotions, thoughts, and fears—to engage with. This is precisely why crisis comes. Until now, we have not known ourselves—who we are, what we truly want, and how to love ourselves. Something has gotten in the way.

The Script Within: Lies We Tell Ourselves

A sixty-seven-year-old man, a lover of nature, a good old Kentucky boy, sits with me in a Vision Fast camp. He's spilling his guts, having struggled for fifty years with messages of shame and self-hatred bequeathed to him by a rigorous church upbringing. An elderly woman, who spent seventy years betraying herself to an abusive husband,

71

finally breaks free at age ninety-two. Both stories speak to immense courage in the face of self-betrayal.

Any person, loved one, or institution who separates us from who we really are betrays us. It happens daily in our schools, government, workplaces, and mass media. Our loved ones—partners, parents, grandparents, siblings, aunts and uncles—collaborate as well. From a young age, a script is delivered that discourages us from knowing who we are.

Sit quietly and listen.
Be seen, not heard.
Make the grade or fail.
Get a job and make something of yourself.
Love me or leave me.
Be a good Christian or suffer in hell.

Simply put, the script says, *You are not enough.* It manipulates us through shame and fear. The *not enough* script comes at us from all directions. As a result, we internalize it, invisible to our own eye. We believe we are not enough and collude with it, seduced by its familiarity. Ubiquitous in the cultural waters, we unknowingly drink it in.

Be more. Do more. Make more money. Get a bigger house. In our negative internalization of these messages, it turns into something like: I'm not smart enough; I can't do that; I'll never make it work; I don't deserve love. When projected onto others, it's: He's a jerk. She's a bitch. He's clueless. Regardless of the target, it's a quiet buzz in our inner system that says we are not okay as we are.

Psychologists call it confabulation: a disturbance of memory, defined as the production of fabricated, distorted, or misinterpreted memories about oneself or the world, without the conscious intention to deceive. It is a voice of self-judgement, a rapacious inner critic, an internalized self-oppression. Unlike other oppressions outwardly identified as racism, sexism, ageism, or anti-Semitism, we rarely see the oppression within ourselves. Yes, it's twisted. It makes no sense. But once we see it, we may rewrite the script.

Core Wounds and Repetition Compulsion

Within the *not enough* script, subtle psychological mechanisms are at work—in how we repeat old relational patterns, how we sabotage ourselves, and how we neglect our most precious relationships. Freud called it the *thanatos*, "death drive": the opposing force to one's creative life force. Coyote trickster is the analogy in native cultures. In *The King Within*, Robert Moore and Douglas Gillette call it "repetition compulsion":

> "By a psychological mechanism termed 'repetition compulsion,' our unconscious compels us, even in adulthood, to repeat the childhood traumas we suffered at the hands of our parents. We recapitulate the same relational patterns imprinted on us when we were young, before we had any Ego structure to speak of and before we had developed any defensible psychological boundaries."

We repeat the hard stuff from childhood. The brother who beat us up, the mother who yelled at us, the teacher who shamed us in front of the class. We rehash these experiences—the shame, the guilt, and fear—in our most primary relationship where it's safe and familiar.

Four times a man marries and divorces essentially the same woman, a version of his raging mother. A woman never develops a significant intimate relationship with a male partner, for no man can compare to the amazing father she had when she was a little girl. A woman constantly complains about her husband. He's this. He's that. She's really beating up on her absent father.

It sounds crazy, and yet it happens all the time. This dynamic is described in detail in Harville Hendrix's book *Getting the Love You Want*, as well as Matt Kahn's YouTube video *Soul Contracts, Twin Flames & Soul Mates Redefined*. Buddhists call it Samsara, repeating the cycle of suffering. Consider it your soul's contract with your partner. It's a way of completing the unfinished business of childhood, to heal in adulthood what was broken in us as children. It is why we come together in partnership—for growth—but only if we are willing to become conscious of the pattern. And when we don't, our relationship blows up on us.

If you were abandoned as a child, you will likely choose an emotionally absent partner. If you grew up with a domineering parent, you may choose an overly assertive partner—or, conversely, take on the dominating role and seek out a partner as a doormat. We unconsciously choose a partner who will do these old replays with us. And then we wonder why we have the same fights with our partners over and over. This is our soul's attempt to get whole. Until we see our patterns, we hurt the way we've been hurt and project the way we were once projected on.

Unconscious to this dynamic, we put on masks and armor our hearts with shields of complacency, apathy, and even cynicism to survive. We resign ourselves to stories like: He'll never change, I'll never be happy, or that's just how he is. And our hearts feel the cost in diminished love, sparse connection, and sometimes estrangement. A woman wakes up panicked at 3 a.m., staring at her husband of twenty years, wondering, *Who is this man I've been married to forever?* What she's not asking is, *Who have I become with this person?*

Bill and the Mask

Bill, a middle-aged man, sits several feet from me. His face is hidden behind a plastic white pantomime mask commonly used in theatre. His body dwarfs the mask. He is a large man. We engage in a process called voice dialogue, where we speak to a part of him directly—in this case, his mask—to reveal an old *not enough* script that's been running him.

"Welcome, Bill's mask," I say.

"Hello," Bill says from behind the mask.

"Can I ask you a few questions?"

"Sure," he says.

"How old were you when you first felt like you had to hide Bill behind the mask?"

"Hmmm…" He thinks. "When he was five."

"What happened then?"

He pauses, reluctant to speak. I wait.

"His mom beat him regularly." He sighs, his barrel chest contracting, and looks away.

I pause, feeling the impact, saying nothing for a moment. "And how did you help Bill deal with that?"

"I made him invisible."

"How?"

"I hid him as much as I could."

"Say more."

"His mom would be drunk and angry and ... I would help him disappear under his bed."

"So, you helped Bill survive?"

"Yes."

"And do you still show up in Bill's life today?"

"Yes, I hide him from his wife."

"How do you do that?"

"Whenever she asks stuff of him, I help him hide and disappear. And she's always in his shit."

"So, you can protect him sometimes, but sometimes you can't?"

"Yes."

"And how's that working for Bill?"

Bill pauses and shakes his head. "She's not happy. And neither am I."

Until now, Bill has feared looking under the mask, fearing a dark truth. By avoiding this truth, he has created his own misery. This is the most painful truth for all of us, to look into the reality that—after thirty, forty, or fifty years of life—we have failed ourselves. Most of us will not look under the mask. It's too painful. Avoiding it makes sense, but it also cheats us of the gifts that await us if we do.

Other Masks We Wear

A working mom wears the Caretaker mask and gives all her energy over to her family before asking anything for herself.

A middle-aged man wears the Nice Guy mask with his wife. "She's going through a lot right now," he says, "I can't ask her for intimacy." And yet it's been two years since they've had sex.

The Martyr says, "He works so hard, how can I expect him to listen to me?"

The Workaholic tries to prove his self-worth through his work and income.

A woman in a sexless marriage wears the mask of Justifier. "Screw him, I'm going to get my needs elsewhere."

The masks are many and endless. To emancipate, we have to take off the mask. Setting it down can be terrifying at first, but soon enough we realize how much easier it is to breathe. Now, we begin to ask ourselves: *Who am I without the mask?*

Rescuer Mask

A week after leaving my wife, I moved into a short-term, furnished executive rental. That first night, I stared at myself in the bathroom mirror brushing my teeth, no one at my side for the first time in twenty-five years. I felt a mix of terror and joy. Being alone scared me more than death itself. All of a sudden, I was sleeping alone, eating alone, coming and going by myself. I cried for what I'd lost. And yet just behind the grief, I was giddy. A calm, clear voice within told me this was how it had to be. It was traumatic and liberating. I battled all the old heartstrings that tugged on me to return home, remaining steadfast. I knew I was on the right path. I had to be alone to face myself honestly for the first time in my adult life.

In the mirror, I saw myself naked; I had taken off my mask. The Rescuer, my preferred mask, had given me a sense of self-worth in caring for my wife that I didn't have within myself. Down in there was the old script of *not enough*. I told myself that if I could help my wife get well, it would make me well. The hidden truth behind my Rescuer mask was that I wanted to rescue myself. With the Rescuer, alongside the Good Guy, the Macho Hero, the Fixer, and the Martyr, I had bandaged my wounds with the false belief that I could save the day. I had worn many masks. There was no way I could make the leap with all those masks on. I had to drop them all.

In a subtle paradox, the hope of being rescued is the ultimate motive of the Rescuer. It is a covertly self-serving, unconscious motivation to be okay by making another okay: pathological altruism. By serving my wife for years without question, I unconsciously sought to repair the part in me that feared doing to her what had been done to me—the child in me who had suffered neglect. These were primal pathological forces beyond love and care, unconsciously driving me to betray myself. Ironically, it only made her worse. In an enabling pattern, I diminished her wellness and empowerment.

That is, until I no longer did. Staring in the mirror, I felt vulnerable and real.

The Cost of Wearing the Mask

Bill takes off the mask. His face is ruddy from emotion and the physical imprint of the mask on his face, the strap marks running across his temples.

"So, Bill, what was it like wearing the mask?" I ask.

"Safe."

"And what else?"

"Shitty."

"How so?"

"I felt like I was dying."

"Say more."

"I was a little boy in a man's body, hiding from momma."

I pause and let the impact of his words settle in. "Are you willing to keep doing that?"

"No," says Bill.

"So, what's next?"

"I have to speak to my wife."

"What will you say?"

"A scared little boy has been running my life. I'm sorry."

"Do you think she'll understand that?"

"Oh yeah." He laughs. "She's been calling me out on that for years."

"And what's different now? Why can you own up to it?"

"Because I know it now. I see it with my own eyes."

"Yes."

A sleeping giant has awoken and come back to life. Energy that has been lost since he was a boy returns to him. The smile on his face is wide and wonderful.

In physically wearing the mask, as I encouraged Bill to do, we claim and amplify the role so that we may own it. We move from unconsciously wearing the mask to saying, "This is my mask, I am the one who puts it on, and I am going to start choosing when to wear it." The mask reveals the unconscious behaviors that obstruct intimacy—when we're being inauthentic in not speaking an important truth or abdicating in a relationship. In exaggerating the mask, we see what we've been hiding from and all that it has cost us.

Owning the Mask

The wearing of masks starts as kids. We seek feedback from our environment, our teachers, and parents. Masks help us get approval and attention, at the very least. The masks include the good kid, the popular kid, the sweet kid, the apathetic loner, or the badass. Even before we've mastered verbal language, we put on masks. The first mask we put on is our own hands.

"Peek a boo." You hid your face, as did the adult playing with you.

What was so wonderful about this?

Ask any child, and he or she will tell you, "I get to pretend. I get to be someone else."

The same is true for adults. We get to be someone else. We get to hide and disappear. Through the mask, we can escape ourselves. We can get safe. And what better way than a mask to avoid a painful truth? A truth about what's not working in your life?

The mask is invisible to us when we're wearing it. Often, it becomes a part of us, no different than our nose or eyes. In our primary relationship, it conforms to who we want our partner to believe we are and who we think he or she wants us to be. Over time, we become the mask. We forget who we are and what we authentically want in relationship. We lose connection to our original spark as a couple. We get cynical about love. We experience a diminished life force. And we resent our partner for making us believe we must wear the mask. Once we remove the mask, we get access to a swell of suppressed energy underneath. In this way, the mask transforms from a marginal protector into a powerful ally.

In removing the mask, our goal is not to banish or reject the parts of our self that have been hidden. We understand that masks are not "bad" unto themselves. They are merely old strategies to get love and be okay that worked as children but no longer work as adults. Instead of banishing, we seek to bring out these hidden parts of ourselves, heal them, and have them on our team as allies. Once made visible, these parts can become our superpowers.

The Rescuer becomes a powerful lover when she gives love to give love and not just to get it. The Perpetrator becomes a healthy self-advocate communicating his needs lovingly and creating clear boundaries. The Workaholic uses his passion for work not to prove his self-worth, but to give his gifts to the world..

Chapter 7

Golden Shadow: The One

*"Until you make the unconscious conscious, it will
direct your life and you will call it fate."*

– Carl Jung

When we leap, we reveal what's underneath the mask—parts of ourselves we cannot see. These are parts that we are unconscious to and repress, parts that we have feared. It could be our self-worth—he will never love me. Or, our trust in others—he's never there for me. This is shadow. The great keeper of the status quo and the *not enough* inside of us. When kept in the dark, shadow keeps us small and falsely safe. It is unconscious and, as Jung says, will direct our lives until we make it conscious.

Shadow

*"… humans come to full consciousness precisely by
shadowboxing, facing their own contradictions, and making
friends with their own mistakes and failings."*

– Richard Rohr, *Falling Upward*

The very nature of being human results in a considerable amount of shadow material, no matter how ideal our upbringing. The socialization process as we grow up is all about taming our wild impulses and forcing us to conform. Anyone who has watched a three-year-old have a public temper tantrum recognizes how painful this process is. In order to reclaim our primal life force energy, we have to jump in the ring and take on our shadow. How do we do that? We go to our edges, the cliffs of our fears. We take off our masks. We challenge the *not enough* script. We explore the dark cave of our disowned self.

For years, I kept my needs in shadow. From childhood, I believed that it was not okay to have needs; they would either be unmet or a burden to others. I was a sensitive boy with busy parents who worked long hours. I feared inconveniencing them. Everyone seemed pre-occupied already. To compensate, I focused outward and attempted to meet the needs of others. I lived by a mantra: *Make others happy, and then I can be happy.* Naturally, I brought this dynamic into my marriage. With my wife's chronic health challenges, she was the perfect person with whom to enter into a soul contract. Ironically, I also became a burden to her.

For some, their shadow is anger. They shut it down, timidly fearing its expression. Others flaunt their anger with an aggressive temper for all the world to see, but they still don't see it themselves. For others, being vulnerable is their shadow. They project a facade of strength into the world, bypassing a precious part of themselves. The continued suppression of an essential part of one's self keeps it in shadow.

In another example of paradox, shadow separates us from parts of our selves so that we may see those parts more clearly. Just as we break down a car into parts to diagnose a problem, dismantling our shadow requires that we take apart the engine that runs our lives. Shadow has this paradoxical purpose. Like our masks, shadow is a protective mechanism that can be a source of awakening when explored. It's only dark as long we *keep* it in the dark. A commonly cited quote by Carl Jung, to whom we owe much of our knowledge of shadow, says, "One does not become enlightened by imagining figures of light, but by making the darkness conscious."

Relationship challenges offer us a remarkable opportunity to step into shadow. If you face your own contradictions, mistakes, and failings, you can grow. Always step at your own pace, but keep stepping. Walk into the parts of yourself that are bursting to be free and expand your life force. These are parts that are alive but lost in pain. Once we bring our shadows into the light, we may discover that our weaknesses can become our strengths. Today, I embrace my needs as precious parts of me that guide me on how to be in relationships with clarity, self-responsibility, and strength—without the fear of losing love or burdening others.

Golden Shadow

> *"Our deepest fear is not that we are inadequate.*
> *Our deepest fear is that we are powerful beyond measure.*
> *It is our light, not our darkness that most frightens us."*

> – Marianne Williamson, *A Return to Love*

On the flip side of shadow is the golden shadow, positive qualities in ourselves that we avoid by projecting them onto others instead of living them ourselves. As Williamson says, it's our light we fear most, not our darkness. To spot golden shadows, notice what you admire in others but don't think you possess. Listen to the self-talk: *Wow, he's so talented. I could never be as good as her. She's so much smarter than me.* In romantic relationship, the Golden Shadow shows up when we say, "She makes me whole," or "He completes me." It's the idea that your partner holds the key to your happiness. In our culture's model of love, it is the promise of The One. A belief system that encourages us to believe we are somehow incomplete, and that the only way to be *whole* is to find the perfect partner who completes us.

Love Me Unconditionally

I sit in a pay to operate massage chair at Denver International Airport, waiting for a flight to New York, A well-dressed woman in her mid-twenties sits in the massage chair next to me. We start talking. She loves her career and travels a lot for work and pleasure. Attractive and financially successful, she manages distribution processes for a major chemical manufacturer. She has many friends and lives a rich life, she says. And yet in our brief conversation, she discloses to me that there is a part of her that is empty.

"It's hard out there. I'm hoping to meet someone soon," she says. "You know, that special someone who will make me feel safe, be there for me, love me unconditionally."

I nod, but I'm unsettled. I breathe into the discomfort I feel in my chest. I don't know why she tells me this. Maybe it's her way of calling herself out, of saying her great life is not so great after all. I feel the anxiety of words that I lived for decades: "… someone who will make me feel safe…" I know the cost of believing, like a dependent child, that my partner could make me feel safe.

Listening to her, I consider how I had sought unconditional love and safety from my wife for years. In doing so, I had avoided responsibility for my own safety and happiness. Seeking the ultimate union in my marriage, I had abandoned my own needs and well-being. While some time has passed since I reversed the old patterns, through the young woman's story, I still feel the heartache of wanting my partner to love me in a way that I had not loved myself.

I look over at the young woman. She's looking away, reflecting.

"That's hard," I say after a while.

"Yes," she says.

The mechanical rotating balls in my massage chair come to a stop. The boarding call for my flight echoes from the airport speakers. I get up and wish her well.

The Burden of "The One"

"We turn to one person to fulfill an endless list of needs.
To be my greatest lover, my best friend, the best parent,
my trusted confidante, my emotional companion, my intellectual equal.
And I am it. I am chosen to be unique. I am indispensable.
I am irreplaceable. I'm the one."

— Esther Perel, *Mating in Captivity*

Perel calls it "monolithic monogamy," the burden of The One. It is a relational construct to compensate for the endemic loneliness of the modern world. Wired for community, the average person has fewer intimate friends, family, and community than ever before. Up until seventy years ago, we often lived close to extended family—aunts, uncles, cousins, siblings, in-laws, parents, and grandparents. And today, many of us have even lost contact with siblings and parents. In the void, our partner, The One, becomes it all. The One is lover, friend, teacher, soulmate, guide, and more, fulfilling roles an entire community once fulfilled. As a wedding officiant, I've often heard in marriage vows: "You will be my guide, my teacher, my companion, my lover, my friend…" At twenty-seven, I spoke similar vows to my fiancé.

How often do we give everything over to The One, believing he or she holds the key to our happiness? In hope of achieving unity with another? And why, in the process, do we abdicate from loving ourselves? We abandon ourselves, believing that's what it truly means to love another person. Unconsciously, it's as if we're saying, "Hold all of my broken self, for I cannot hold myself."

Heterosexual men do this when they outsource their tenderness to their female partner. She's the only one to whom he believes he can reveal his soft side, a part that is culturally disparaged as unmanly. And when she withdraws her love from him, he loses a precious part of himself and feels powerless. It's a shit storm waiting to happen, with men often getting violent as a result.

This is not to say that we shouldn't turn to one another with needs and wants. Of course, we should. But we need to know the difference between outsourcing parts of ourselves and cultivating those parts within. In the right balance, a man might say, she inspires me to be a more tender man with myself, my kids, and my friends.

Over the years, as we give ourselves away in a relationship; we get so embedded in one another that we lose one another. We struggle to speak simple truths like, I'd like to be closer or I'd like to work on our relationship. We grow apart. Instead of living vitally together, what lives is the *unlived* life of the couple. It's the ghost of who we once were, a potentiality floating between two estranged hearts.

How We Lose One Another in Relationship

What happens? How do we lose one another? Simply stated, we forget how to replenish the source of our passion. We become confined with little independence and many shared assets—home, finances, and possibly children. Blissful union from the early years becomes marital suffocation of the middle and later years. Like furniture in a crowded house, we wander around among the assets, failing to cultivate the true sources of happiness such as our passion, mystery, dreams, or Eros, that exotic part of us that is deeply curious about our partner.

> *"There are parts of our personal story that are top secret.*
> *They are off limits; we do not dare reveal them to anyone.*
> *All this holding back makes us believe that our partner also has*
> *no further mysteries to reveal. At this point, Eros begins to recoil."*

> – Prem Baba, *From Suffering to Joy*

At some point in the journey, we make a bargain. We trade passion for security. And if we are courageous enough to acknowledge the loss of passion, we resist working on it, fearing that it may diminish the little security we have—even if it's built on years of betrayals and unspoken truths. This is marriage today for most couples. According to psychologist Ty Tashiro, author of *The Science of Happily Ever After*, seventy percent of married couples are not in healthy, happy marriages.

On the flip side, we are quite close with lots of passion and fireworks in the early years of a relationship. We are often even hungry to give up our freedom for connection. We abandon our sovereignty for the enchantment of The One. We value our partner greatly, energized by him or her. We do special things for one another. We consider his or her feelings and how we can maintain closeness and passion. But years later, as we get more secure with one another, things change. We take one another for granted. We go from high connection to low connection. We end up where we said we'd never go, where our parents may have arrived—with little connection and an impermeable security. We ask ourselves: *How can I feel so trapped with the one I was so in love with? What happened?*

What happened was we lost ourselves in a misleading romantic model of love early on. We did precisely as modern romance said we should. We abandoned ourselves for one another. We forgot who we were for the sake of "complete union." I became her and she became me, cultivating a womb to return to in one another—the primal "urge to merge." For a short time, we achieved the greatest bliss our culture promotes as the ultimate end game of love—the loss of self in the other, with fireworks, sex, security, and passion. But nobody ever told us we couldn't live there for the next twenty years.

Eventually, we have to come home to ourselves. We are left stranded without a post honeymoon model of relationship. We can no longer give away our sovereignty as a couple just because nobody taught us otherwise. Even if they had, we might have chosen the same path, pleasure over truth. Eventually, crisis says, "Enough, no more, remove the masks worn to escape the hard truth of how far we've drifted." But fearing even more pain, we blame one other instead of acknowledging the false foundation we had to start with.

> *"Though no one notices at the time, in-love-ness obliterates the humanity of the beloved. One does a curious kind of insult to another by falling in love with him, for we are really looking at our projection of God, not at the other person."*
>
> – Robert A. Johnson, *Owning Your Own Shadow*

As Johnson says, we are humans after all—not Gods. When all functions—friend, lover, soulmate, and more—get outsourced to one's partner, it's a romantic death blow. A level of burden on The One doomed to fall short. Fill my emptiness and then I can hate you when you fail. After a while, our inner system rebels and we lose each other, or it all blows up. Instead, we must ask, how may we hold the God energy in ourselves? How may we reclaim our wholeness, so we may share it with our beloved as a gift, instead of a burden?

Love in the Media and Patho-Adolescence

Surely you heard this story from a young age. Once upon a time there was a boy. He met a girl. He liked her a lot. She liked him. They fell in love. They got married. They had children. And they lived happily ever after. Most of us have been living in the shadow of this story since before puberty. In pursuit of our own "happily ever after," we embrace the myth of The One.

"Love is putting someone else's needs before yours," Olaf the snowman says to Anna in the Disney film *Frozen*. When Jake at age fifteen said these words to me after I left his mom, I felt he was implying that I had failed her. But I knew better.

"They forgot one critical word," I said to him. "That one word is *sometimes*."

From a young age, our media-saturated culture feeds us an adolescent model of relationship—*always* meeting another's needs, regardless of the cost. Give it all over to The One and love will be yours. In movies, novels, and pop songs, the messages flood our psyche throughout adolescence and adulthood. "You... I would die for you," Prince says in the song "I Would Die 4 U."

Self-abandonment to another is romantically intoxicating, high chemistry, and big business. Who can deny that? Romantic love crushes mature love at the box office. It has an allure and appeal of which Romantics have been singing since the late eighteenth century. Who doesn't love a good love story? Ahhh, the endorphins flood us— euphoric, epiphanous, and yet ephemeral.

Dare I deny the value of romantic love? Absolutely not. Fireworks, sparks, and physical chemistry are the electricity that light us up.

Exciting and exhilarating, we'd live there forever if we could. But the less sexy truth is that electricity needs wiring. And wiring needs framing built on a concrete foundation. To deny this is to live in what author and Franciscan friar Richard Rohr calls a "patho-adolescent" (pathologically adolescent) culture, in which older married couples live in the hangover of the fireworks of their early years.

Beyond patho-adolescence is mature, sovereign relationship built on a solid foundation and framework that makes it possible for the electricity to fly for years. It starts with healthy self-relationship and goes from there. Each of us can hold ourselves so that we may stand strong for one another. Each of us lives knowing that we can't expect fulfillment with one another if we have not attained a measure of it in ourselves. Of course, we rarely come to romantic relationships as rock-solid individuals skilled in the art of self-mastery. Instead, we must embrace self-relationship while in a partnered relationship, where it's so easy to lose ourselves. For those entangled in marriage or a relationship, that may not be possible. Having completely forgotten who you are, you may need to be alone to truly come home to yourself.

Chapter 8

Coming Home to One's Self

"When there is nothing left to lose, we find the true self—the self that is whole, the self that is enough, the self that no longer looks to others for definition, or completion, or anything but companionship on the journey."

– Elizabeth Lesser, *Broken Open*

What does it mean, to come home to one's self? I've asked clients over the years. Answers have ranged from, "I can relax and be comfortable in who I am," to "I can trust myself." We all inherently want this, yet so few of us have it. In its absence, I hear clients say, "I want to be clear on what I want"; "I want to show up in life with absolute confidence"; "I want to know how to get love." When we realize what we're lacking, the sense of emptiness can be overwhelming.

We may attempt to get answers from a blog, a Google search, a dream, an ayahuasca trip, or a workshop. All can offer some relief, but eventually you must take a sustained trip to the inner world. In my experience, that only happens by engaging with your challenges consistently, going to the places you fear to go, and staying committed to your work. "Stare into the abyss long enough and the abyss will stare back at you" (Nietzsche). That's the eye contact a soul warrior thrives on. It is there that we may rewire old beliefs and fears. It is there that we may disentangle relational patterns that no longer serve us.

Grief and the Little Boy

Within days of moving into my executive rental, broken up by the prospect of my marriage's end, I went to the well—the true source of my well-being, my relationship with myself. The next few months and years would be a tutelage in healthy self-reliance, an arduous restructuring of my internal being.

It began with grieving the loss of my family, who had been my life's foundation. As challenging as my marriage was, most of my self-identity had been built from our twenty plus years together. Marisa and I had always had a deep connection, in addition to a closeness with our son. To fully grieve, I had to go back to the place before I met my wife, before we had our son. I had to go all the way back to when I was a little boy.

As grief took hold of me in my new apartment, it was the little boy who showed up. An inner child. He was who I was crying for, not merely my wife. He was the source of it all. He still sought the love that he hadn't gotten as a boy. Soft and super sensitive, he felt the sting of growing up with a physically confrontational older brother and often busy, working parents. The little boy spent hours on end alone. He lived in the shadow of his parents' affection-impoverished marriage, frequented by fights about money. Rarely, if ever, was love expressed between them; in the boy's perception, it was mostly acrimony or apathy.

Years later, that little boy in me was determined to do better. He would love in a way that they had not. Guided by the boy's imperative, as a young man I took the Beatles' lyrics to heart: "All You Need Is Love." I would love my wife in the way my father did not love my mother. If I had love with her, all would be well regardless of the cost. Seeking to meet the child's unmet needs for love, connection, and visibility in my marriage, the little boy came up empty-handed. He knew it. And now, he turned to me.

What would it mean to love the boy and be responsible for his needs? It would mean going to the place where traditional manhood said, "No!" The hardest place imaginable—to the depths of my own brokenness. To grief. And so, the tears came. I physically felt the boy—his body, his memories. I felt the physical confrontations with my big brother, pinned down with his knees on my arms. I remembered the unhinged verbal rage of my father, and my mother's evening absences from home to avoid a long work commute. With the tears came the repair of old cells in my body, the healing of stuck emotions and energies. To love the little boy fully was to fully love myself, to rewrite the *not enough* script, to remove the mask and rewire old neural pathways. It was the work of becoming a father to the boy, the father he never had.

Connecting the dots, it became clear that I had been seeking with my wife the visibility that I didn't have growing up. Twenty-three years later, the cost of doing so became too much. I needed more than just love. I also needed emotional safety, trust, autonomy, and sovereignty. And that had to be cultivated within myself first. Once done, it would never be lost. Only apart from my wife could I know who I was. Only outside of the enmeshed unit we'd become could I heal the boy and become the man. It was a confronting, honoring, and unwinding of all that had taken me up to this moment in my life.

Re-Opening the Channel of Love

> *"Grief needs boundaries. Despair knows no boundaries."*
>
> – Michael Gurian, *The Invisible Presence*

To meet the child is to come home to one's self, full circle, in order to integrate the hurt parts and heal. It is how we re-open the channels of love within. It is how we get back to our natural health and equilibrium. Through grief, we hold the container of what is broken in us. We meet the wounds within. We initiate and become emotionally self-responsible adults. Through grief, we become whole.

Grief is the hardest of human emotions, but our general culture has little understanding of its healing value. Even though Dr. Elisabeth Kübler-Ross' book *On Death and Dying*, published in 1969, gave us the language of the five stages of grief (denial and isolation, anger, bargaining, depression, and acceptance), we often still avoid grief at all costs, mistaking it for weakness. Most of us only give ourselves permission to grieve when a loved one passes. The loss of a long-term relationship or the death of a part of our self can be just as painful. The truth is, only the strong can grieve. Grief is the hard rain washing the muck out of one's soul. Without it, we cannot heal.

The Source of Self-Betrayal: The Wounded Child

"Find the child who wants to strike out and you will be in control of evolving negative emotions without repressing them, but expressing them constructively and learning from them. Find the area in which you resent not being taken care of, not being given all you want. Once you are aware of the reason for all this anger, you will be able to humor yourself, because you will see the preposterous demands of the child in you."

– Eva Pierrakos, *The Pathwork of Self-Transformation*

The child had many demands of my wife; he wanted touch, connection, reassurance, and love. And he often wanted to strike out at her, resentful that he was not getting his needs met. During my marriage, I did not have the tools to identify him. Yet I often felt like a whiny little boy was inside of me. It was only when I left home that I understood a deep internal split had lived within me, between the boy and the man. While I could easily scapegoat my wife for not meeting my needs, the boy targeted me for enabling it. I could not be happy in such a fractured state. Healing that rift meant first tending to the boy. Only then could I show up as an adult.

Is there such a split in you? Is there such a child? Whether you acknowledge it or not, you have some memory of the child you once were—except in cases of severe trauma. Many of those memories speak to times when your needs were not met. Perhaps your father was gone a lot or your mother was overbearing. As adults, we commonly hear others say, "My mother never... My father never..." Instead of acknowledging our unmet needs, we typically project them onto our partner. In this way, we either deny our partner what we didn't get as kids, or expect them to magically meet our needs without saying what they actually are.

Susan and Maxine

"A hero is one who takes on the damage of his or her lineage."

– Terry Real, Author and Psychotherapist

Susan loves Maxine. Susan knows she is an amazing woman. Maxine shows up in all areas of their lives—from their kids to their relationship, house chores, and income contribution. Still, Susan feels there's something not enough in Maxine.

"It's as if she is so perfect, and I know this is horrible… I think I'd only admit this to you. It's as if I need to cut her down to build myself up," Susan says. "Sometimes I say things to her, and I don't feel like it's me talking."

"Who is it, then?" I ask.

"I don't know. But I find myself saying things to her like, 'Why don't you love me more? I need more from you!' Sounds pathetic, as I say it."

"Yeah, I hear you. Not something you're proud of."

"No."

While the difference between therapy and coaching in this moment can be subtle, I ask her about her childhood. As a coach, I am less concerned about her past than how it shows up in the present. How can Susan see her behavior, of which she's not proud, is within her power to change?

In moments, Susan tells me that as a child, her mom had often said to her, "You need to listen! I know best!" If she didn't listen, her mom's voice would increase in volume or Susan would be sent to bed without dinner. She felt invisible to her mother.

And here Susan is, years later, with similar words coming out of her mouth toward her partner: "Listen to me! You need to listen!" It's as if Susan is a little girl fighting her own invisibility with her partner.

This is the child with unmet needs. At first, she is floored at the realization.

"How is that possible? It makes total sense—how could I not see this?"

"Because you didn't need to, until now."

She nods. She gets it. Moving ahead, Susan fights the impulse of the old voice. She realizes that her beef is not with Maxine, but the child within. She understands that until now, a primal force has compelled her to deprive Maxine of what she herself didn't get from her mother. One unmet need is driving her to create another. A reactive imperative to continue a cycle deep in her lineage—from her mother to her grandmother, and to her great grandmother and beyond. Old programming that had Susan denying to Maxine the visibility that her mother had denied her. For years, she had been in a relationship with Maxine, unaware of it. It had made her miserable, until now.

Mold in the Dark

Why does the child run us in difficult moments? Simply put, because at a random age, we are told it is "Time to grow up and become an adult." Unmet childhood needs get stuffed in the closet at eighteen, or younger. In the absence of any meaningful rites of passage from childhood to adulthood, we never face the child's unmet needs. And when those needs continue unmet, we repeat them in our relationships as adults. Repetition compulsion, again. How often do we hear it said, "He's a child in a man's body"?

Ironically, the strategy of shutting down the child to become an adult interferes with our maturation into healthy adults. As a child, shutting down needs was effective and helped us survive. But for the adult, doing so is treason. Like mold in a dark container, left to fester and swell, it breeds shadow. In the gap, we project the child's complaints onto our partner. That is, until we wake up to the child's demands.

Child Versus Adult Needs

> *"The perpetuation of false [child] needs creates any number of destructive conditions within the soul of a person ... Real [adult] needs never require others to comply and 'give it to you.'"*

– Eva Pierrakos, *The Pathwork of Self-Transformation*

When the child is running us, we demand things of our partner. I need her to listen to me. I need him to pay more attention to me. I need her to love me more. I hear clients talk like this all the time. Underneath the adult's voice is the complaint of the child.

Mature adults do not make demands of a partner that he or she must give to them. Instead, they communicate a willingness to responsibly self-advocate, often as simple as lovingly speaking a request: "I would like to spend more time together." Healthy adults understand that in every complaint is an implicit request. We do not project onto our partner what we refuse to step into ourselves. To become self-responsible, we need to separate unmet child needs from authentic adult needs. Childhood needs cannot be met by our partner; she or he is not our parent. Nothing kills attraction and Eros like a projected child-parent dynamic. The child's needs must be met by you.

Below are a few examples to illustrate the difference between statements spoken from unmet child needs versus authentic adult needs. Authentic adult needs are requests spoken in clear, direct language, whereas the child's complaints are often ambiguous, implied, or sideways.

STATEMENTS OF NEEDS

UNMET CHILD	AUTHENTIC ADULT
I need you to listen to me.	*I want to talk to you.*
I need you to pay more attention to me.	*I would like to connect with you.*
I need you to love me.	*I want to experience more love with you.*
You never listen to me	*I have something important to tell you.*

Being an Adult When Childhood Needs Arise

Sandy is sitting at the dinner table with her partner. Suddenly, she's feeling insecure. She has no idea why. Still, the thoughts come—*Does he love me? Is he really there for me?*

Have you ever been in a mood where, out of the blue, you're feeling uncertain about your relationship with your partner? You haven't spent much quality time together in a while. You wonder if your partner notices or even cares. You ask the same question as Sandy: *Does he even love me anymore?* A part of you wonders, *What's come over me?*

Here, you have an opportunity. You can catch yourself. Instead of opening your mouth to your partner, you can pause and be silent. You can go within—to the feeling, to your inner child—and revolutionize your relationship and your life. Own the insecurity like an adult. Don't project it onto your partner. Connect with yourself. Pause and take a breath, and feel the insecurity in your body. Where does it live in you? Be with the feeling. Rarely do we do this. Instead, we project it onto our partner, try to fix it, or avoid the feeling.

Notice if the child within is triggered. Reach out to her.

What's going on, little one?

I'm scared, the child says.

What are you scared of?

Whatever the child's answer, understand that the child simply seeks to be seen in a way that he or she wasn't when you were an actual child. As much as we may resist this process, this is a powerful moment that can transpire in minutes. Here, you can build the inner muscles to reverse decades of old emotional programming. Seeing the child is a profound way to heal old wounds, self-regulate (be okay on your own), and be in healthy self-relationship. The love you give to the child opens you up to give love to your partner. The love to the child enables the child to be okay. Sound insane? Maybe. But once you go into it, it's real as the furniture in front of you. Yes, you can be with yourself in this way. You may say to the child, *It's okay. I'm okay. We're okay. I'm here for you.*

After that, you can return to your partner as an adult. You are clear. The child is not running you. Maybe you even remember, *Oh yeah. I need connection, not approval.* And you ask your partner to connect.

"We haven't had a lot of time together lately. I miss you. Can you take a moment to see me?"

When you make the request, your partner may say, "What's wrong? Did I upset you?"

You can say, "No, I just want to be with you."

Wow, okay, your partner may think. *I can respond to that—a desire for connection. I'm in, me too.* And he recognizes he's in the room with an adult, not a child. That's sexy. Nothing enhances attraction, Eros, and relational energy like an adult speaking his or her own authentic needs. When you separate child and adult needs, you are a king or a queen commanding your relational landscape.

Adult Versus Child Needs: A Roadmap for Adult Relationships

In looking at child needs versus adult needs, we can illuminate old patterns of behavior—how we react, self-betray, and stumble into the same old relational conflicts. Being in a relationship helps us see our unmet child's needs by amplifying them and reflecting them back at us. Our partner presents a great mirror; this is what I spoke of prior as our soul contract. Relationships offer a great opportunity to live from our authentic adult needs. This is the deepest work. But we must put it into action. Look in the dark corners of your psyche, and meet the scared child there peeking back at you.

When we look at how we are acting, what we are asking for in a relationship, we may know where the need is coming from—the child or the adult. Below is a roadmap of authentic adult needs versus unmet childhood needs. Consider the pairs as opposite polarities on a spectrum. At any moment, we may be somewhere on the spectrum. In heated moments, we often regress to the needs of the child. This often triggers a similar regression in our partner. Pretty soon, we've got two wounded kids screaming at each other. When the dust settles, we are often left scratching our heads. Who was that talking? It sure as heck wasn't me.

The key is to work with where you are at, not to judge yourself for not being where you want to go. Master one pair, just like one language, and the rest becomes easier.

Unmet Child	Authentic Adult
Avoids self-relationship	Cultivates healthy self-relationship
Seeks to complete another in relationship	Seeks congruence and mutuality in relationship
Avoids or instigates conflict	Grows through conflict
Seeks a compass in partner	Has a strong inner compass
Projects "The One" onto partner	Owns golden shadow of "The One"
Acts in power over/under (control)	Acts in power with (sovereignty)
Seeks approval of partner	Seeks connection with partner
Wants permission	Engages in communication
Fears loneliness	Enjoys aloneness

The Gift of the Child

"The gifts are near the wounds. In order to get to the gifts, you have to go near the wounds."

– Michael Meade, *Fate and Destiny*

In psychotherapy, we often hear the term "core wounds" to describe the child's unmet needs. Wound is apropos when we first feel into what we didn't get as a child. But as we advance in our growth and integrate the pain of childhood, we no longer see unmet child needs as wounds, deficit, or anything to eradicate. Instead, we understand that we need those old parts to transform into healthy adults. We are grateful to the child, reconnecting to a lost part of our core self, as we grow confident in our ability to hold ourselves.

The child's wounds become the adult's strengths, our soul's teachings, the seeds of our sovereign self. We learn to parent the inner child who no longer runs us. As the child's wounds heal, we are no longer identified by them. We begin to feel and ascend into a higher vibrational frequency of self-trust and inner authority. Our inner compass strengthens and guides us irrevocably to a solid adult self, independent of what we once believed our partner had to be for us.

We are free in a way like we've never been before. The fear of losing our primary relationship no longer feels like life or death. Sure, the loss may hurt, but it alone is not our reason for staying in relationship. We want more and seek congruence in a partner who wants more as well. We seek to be bigger and enriched in partnership instead of falsely completed. We live in the truth that no nobody can give us what we cannot give ourselves. Anything less feels like a low-level pursuit.

The integrated child also offers us the great gifts of natural joy, spontaneity, and innocence, as only a child can embody. The child part of us, when guided by a wise adult, provides a spark of excitement in life—a sense of vitality that, as adults, we often lack. The child gives us access to our dreams and wholeness. With the healthy child's energy alive in us, we get access to a vast reservoir of energy that was lost, energy that will enrich our lives and relationships like never before.

Summary of Strategies

Moving from Unmet Child Needs to Authentic Adult Needs

- Commit to self-regulation (being okay on your own) and self-observation in relationships.
- Be with a partner also willing to self-observe and regulate.
- Know when the child is running you.
- Engage with the child's unmet needs.
- Know the Adult-Child Need Spectrum.
- Give healthy love freely based on adult needs.

Chapter 9

The Gifts of Sovereignty

"From the moment I could talk I was ordered to listen."

– Cat Stevens, *Father and Son*

Sovereignty. It's not a word we hear often in our culture. That is not surprising, as we don't live in a sovereign culture. Sovereignty is the ability to direct one's life in integrity with the knowledge of one's authentic identity and needs. It is one of the great gifts available to us after taking the leap.

Unfortunately, as children, we aren't usually encouraged to discover who we are or what we need. Instead, we are given rules and orders. We are told to comply or face the punishment. This is the socialization process that I brought up earlier. It is painful, and pushes much of our sovereign independence down into shadow. Some of the messages we are given that cripple our sovereignty are as follows:

Sit down and listen.
Study hard and get good grades.
Go to college and get a good job.
Build a career and be happy.
Settle down and get married.

Buy a house and have a family.
Save and have a good retirement.

As we enter sovereignty in adulthood, we unwire from a culture that confines us with its orders. Our personal directives emanate from our own inner authority. We learn to trust the generative voice within that says: *Know what you need, know who you are, be in healthy self-relationship*. We live empowered with the truth that we alone are responsible for the shape of our lives. And while some of us come into the world with more resources than others, we all get to decide what to do with what we have. Consider this Lakota parable.

The Creator gathered all of Creation and said, "I want to hide something from the humans until they are ready for it. It is the realization that they create their own reality."

The eagle said, "Give it to me, I will take it to the moon."

The Creator said, "No. One day they will go there and find it."

The salmon said, "I will bury it on the bottom of the ocean."

"No. They will go there too."

The buffalo said, "I will bury it on the Great Plains."

The Creator said, "They will cut into the skin of the Earth and find it even there."

Grandmother Mole, who lives in the breast of Mother Earth, and who has no physical eyes but sees with spiritual eyes, said, "Put it inside of them."

And the Creator said, "It is done."

For a sovereign individual, the realization that we create our own lives is empowering. We relish the freedom to do so apart from conventional cultural narratives, and sit on the throne of our unique sense of well-being. We develop the self-trust to reject the cultural myths fed to us by Hollywood, Wall Street, and Main Street—that success is only about material wealth or public fame. We are no longer controlled by the media and its incessant message that we aren't enough, but can be if we purchase x, y, or z. Instead, what drives our movement through life is the clear vision and understanding of who we authentically are, independent of who others want us to be. Our media is no longer external, but a listening within.

As sovereigns, we know that success is a private idea, deeply embedded within one's self. We don't assume that the successful TV actor is thriving. He may be like an acquaintance of mine who lives stressed out about finding his next good acting job, haunted by the question, *What have you been in lately?* Often, the most "successful" people, running hard to preserve their wealth, are merely replicating the low-level instinct to survive.

When you have rewritten the script of *not enough*, you believe in your intrinsic self-worth, independent of how you perform. Your self-worth may be as simple as knowing you're a good person; you're a loving person; you have gifts for others. To arrive here, you have weathered the storms of your own growth. This is why I believe it is imperative that we start teaching sovereignty to our children from a young age.

Sovereignty Versus Control

"It's easier to build strong children than to repair broken men."

– Frederick Douglas

As parents, my wife and I quickly learned that it was best to give our son choices rather than to order him around. Raising him, we saw an innate imperative in him to be sovereign.

"Jake, it's time to come home for dinner," I often said from the back patio door.

He was five years old and lost in the world of play in our community area, a large square of green grass surrounded by townhomes. It was an area free of cars, so he and the other kids had the freedom to play outside as they chose.

"Jake!" I said again, stepping into our small fenced yard. From the slight turn of his head toward me while running, I knew he heard me.

As if he could make me go away, he looked away and kept running. *Little rascal.* I chuckled inside.

"Time to come in!"

"No! I'm playing!" he said from a short distance.

"Come here, let's talk."

Fifteen seconds later, the fence gate clicked as he ran into our yard, sweating and winded.

"What, Daddy?" he said in his cute high-pitched voice.

"It's time for dinner."

"I'm not hungry!"

"You have a choice. You can come home now or in ten minutes. Which is it?"

"No! I don't want to come in!" He stomped his foot and threw his hands down, face contorting.

"You don't have to come in now. I gave you a choice. Now or ten minutes? It's your choice. So, which do you like better? If you don't choose, then I will."

"Ten minutes."

"Okay." I looked him in the eyes. "You made the choice. So that means when I call you in ten minutes, you will come in without discussion. Okay?"

"Okay." And he was off to the races, back to the central green with the other kids. Ten minutes would seem like forever in kid time.

I tell this story because it speaks to sovereignty. By giving my son a choice, I honored his natural impulse to influence his reality. While it was a small choice, he was still able to have a part in when he came home.

As with many kids, my son's desire to have his inner authority honored was strong from a young age. "I do it!" he often said, as early as age three. Whether it was opening his own car door or pushing the elevator button in a building, the words came. I remember thinking, *Now that's a healthy sovereign child.* It made me proud to see that come out in him, and to be an ally for him to cultivate that ability. Through my son's natural impulses, I saw how sovereignty is within us from birth, a natural part of our human development. But rarely do we, as parents, see this. Instead, we see something else—disobedience.

Why is it that we don't honor our children's sovereignty, their natural will to make their own choices? I believe it's because we were never taught as kids to honor it in ourselves. When we have an essential strength in ourselves denied, even scorned, it goes into shadow. From there, as we've discussed, its influence over us and our relationships is usually damaging. We find ourselves automatically denying things to our children or partners that we wish we'd have gotten as kids. Out of this confusion grows sovereignty's evil twin: control. Sovereignty builds strong adults, whereas control creates needy children.

In relationships, we can cultivate sovereignty at the simplest level when we give up trying to control or fix our partner. We may try to influence them, but we are willing to trust what they need. Of course, being with a sovereign partner means they're willing to do the same for you.

Will we raise our children to become sovereign adults or controlling adult children? Even at five, we must plant the seeds. Often, it's not until the crisis of mid-life that we understand that we control very little but influence just about everything. Without offering our kids a model of the sovereign, we deprive them of a healthy model of self-relationship. And yet, many adults fumble their way through life without knowing themselves or their gifts. As a result, we have a world where forty- and fifty-year-olds are wondering, *Why did my marriage blow up? How did I end up in this job for ten years? Who am I?*

Becoming One's Authentic and Powerful Self

One of the great gifts of meeting the initiatory journey is sovereignty— the becoming of one's authentic and powerful self. A sovereign individual has worked deeply with her wounded parts and shadows, and from there, she discovers her authentic needs and identity. She understands when the adult is running her versus the child. She no longer builds her identity on the expectations of others. She cultivates a knowledge of who she is, aligned with her gifts and desires. She seeks to do good for others. The initiatory journey is one of creating Generative Kings and Queens in the world.

Discovering one's needs, desires, and identity requires 360-degree vision—the seeing of the larger landscape of one's life, instead of just a narrow path hemmed in by fear and control. To get there, we have to sort through a lot of distractions—news, social media, misguided advice—and old internal patterns. In this process, we may cultivate qualities of the sovereign.

Key Sovereign Qualities

- Directs her life in integrity with her authentic identity, needs, and life priorities.
- Has a faith and trust in her gifts.
- Is resilient with conflict, fear, and the unknown.
- Has a strong inner authority.
- Has a regular practice of self-care.
- Does not betray himself or wear masks for the sake of others.
- Has a profound engagement with his life force.
- Lives in connection with a cause, community, or spiritual path bigger than himself.
- Enters relationship with a sovereign partner.

Sovereign Love: A Love that Expands Our Light

Contrary to seeking power over a partner, a sovereign individual seeks power with a partner. He or she gives love to give love, and not just to get love. His ability to give love emanates from the love he has within himself. This inner love expands with his partner and does not diminish her. He does not expect to be completed by her. He knows that's an unreasonable expectation and, ultimately, his own responsibility. Nonetheless, he feels bigger and richer in her presence because she is confident in her own value, and can reflect back to him what's already within him. It could be as simple as: "I love how she reminds me to stop my constant doing and to just be; I love how she helps me get outside into nature." A sovereign partner helps you to become your most beloved self.

Sovereign partners empower one another to be in healthy self-relationship, be it as simple as going to the gym or visiting with friends. A sovereign couple is invested in the truth of one another's aliveness. There is a mutuality of such truth. Each wants the other's personal truth, knowing the gifts of mutual congruence—anything less feels compromised. Heather knew this when she first called me. Something had to change in her relationship, and she was the one to bring it up.

Who Am I?

Heather phones me and her voice is charged. She and her husband Thomas have two kids, twelve and fifteen.

"He's emotionally checked out," she says. "While he's involved as a father, it's like he goes through the motions. And as a couple, our spark is gone." She pauses, feeling the effect of her words. A moment later, she continues, "For me, it's crazy because there are so many things I want to do, places to travel, adventures to have—but he's content to just sit at home. He gives everything over to work and there's little left for us. It's as if all he has to contribute is his paycheck. And that's enough, in his mind."

"Maybe that's a bit harsh?" I say.

She acknowledges that, but the feeling is still there. She wants to up their game. She wants to be with a man who has opinions and desires. A man who has a connection with his own well-being. She asks me to see him as a client. I check in with her to make sure she's in her sovereign, and not just trying to control.

"I think you could help him, Stuart," she says, "and that would help us both. I'm willing to do my part." She is asking for what she wants, a clear sign of her sovereignty. She seeks connection with him, not his approval. She tells me she often feels like his mother, and is aware that's not a good dynamic.

A week later, Thomas sits in my office, his face blank, his eyes expressionless. As we begin to talk, it's clear that he's grappling with a big question that overwhelms him. He is in his late forties. A big unknown troubles him. He understands that the future of his marriage hinges on the answer. His children are confused by his absent behavior, and are watching closely to see what he does. He speaks in a monotone, vacant inside like a ghost.

"Who am I?"

The weight of his question hangs in the air. I am a silent witness.

I know Thomas' story. It is typical of many men. He has spent most of his life doing—focused on work, family, success, money, and tasks. He has always provided well for his family, trying to be a good man and a good father. Even though he is playing by all the old rules, things are not working out for him. He's aware Heather is unhappy. Sadly, this is true for many women today who, seeking more emotional connection from their husbands, initiate seventy percent of all divorces. Thinking things are fine, this leaves most men baffled.

"My marriage is blowing up. Heather wants more from me. And I don't know what to tell her," he says.

"Heather thinks you're emotionally checked out," I say. "She cannot feel your presence as a man in the house."

He nods his head, knowing it's true. He is disturbed by this. He replays a typical conversation at home. It rings true, based on what Heather has already told me.

"What do you want to do this weekend?" she asks him.

"Whatever you want," he says.

"Where do you want to go for our vacation?"

"You choose, I'm fine."

"I always thought I could make her happy by giving her choices," he says.

Instead, she interprets this as apathy. She feels like she is living with a zombie, not an energized partner. He abdicates emotionally and he doesn't know what he feels most of the time. When she says *enough*, he wakes up to his own emptiness. Now, he's in my office.

As Thomas speaks, I think to myself, *What a cruel question for him*. Who can really answer, *Who am I?* Few people, if any. This is not a sovereign question. It's the wounded, overwhelmed child speaking. Sitting with him, I feel compassion for his struggle, and offer him a way to get a foothold on things.

"Thomas, consider reframing your original question. Instead of 'Who am I?' ask yourself, 'What makes me come alive?'"

He pauses and looks at me. "Hmmmm," he tones.

"And?"

He shrugs his shoulders.

"Do you know what I mean by what makes you come alive?"

"Not really."

"Alive, excited. What do you love to do?"

"I don't know. I don't spend much time thinking about these things."

"Thomas, if you were told you had six months to live, what would you do tomorrow?"

"Get all my affairs in order. Make sure my family was taken care of."

"Is that it? Are there any experiences you'd want to have, things you'd want to do, people to see, places you'd want to go?"

"Parks," he mumbles.

"What?"

"Parks."

"Parks. What about parks?"

"Yosemite. Yellowstone. The Grand Canyon."

"And?"

"I'd want to go see them."

"On your own? With your family? How would you make it happen?"

"I'd take my kids out of school and go with my family."

"Keep going. How would you do it?"

"I'd get a van, pack us up, and visit all the parks I've always wanted to see."

"Yes! Say more. Why the parks?"

He continues on about his fascination with geology and land formations. How he's never said much to his family about it all, figuring it would bore them. I pull more out of him, fascinated at his extensive geological knowledge. Blood returns to his face. In fifteen minutes, the blank of *Who am I?* begins to get filled in.

The reframe from the abstract, *Who am I?* to the concrete *six months to live* inquiry gets Thomas from a daunting unknown to a known. The known de-escalates Thomas' fear of the unknown. It gets him back to a sense of self, from which he relaxes. After further prompting, he begins to speak about his love for his wife and family, and how he always thought providing for them was the best way to show his love for them.

"They need more. They need you."

"I know," he says.

Through what he knows, Thomas accesses what he did not know. In time, he can begin to even welcome the unknown instead of protecting against it. This is sovereignty—the ability to access one's knowing and inner authority.

Selfing Versus Self-Judgement

With sovereignty, we come home to ourselves and our self-trust. Sovereignty sits in the deep seat of faith, in the ability to trust one's self. Engaging an unknown and feeling it or reframing it, you may get back to yourself. I call this the act of "selfing," aligning with yourself. The opposite is fragmenting, losing yourself. This is when you reject a part of yourself. Most often, this occurs with emotions. A voice inside of us says, *I shouldn't be sad*, or *I shouldn't be mad*. It's not the emotion that causes stress as much as the layer of self-judgement between you and the emotion.

In judging our emotions, we critique our value as a person. Ironically, this has the effect of distorting the emotion, causing us even more stress. Once we remove the judgement, we may feel the emotion, receive its message, or allow it to pass. Self-acceptance is kryptonite to our inner critic. The voice of *not enough* cannot survive in an inner ecosystem of love and trust. It is our sovereign choice what we do with our emotions, not whether or not they happen.

In his book *The Inner Matrix*, author and coach Joey Klein speaks to how emotions have a neurological lifespan of ninety seconds. If we can avoid attaching thoughts for ninety seconds, we can move past an emotion. To do so, pause and take a multitude of breaths; often, that alone is enough to break an old cycle. At the threshold of the unknown, we have a choice: welcome it or fear it.

How Self-Love Benefits Partnership

"No resisting, no grasping, we are free."

— A friend on her ideal relationship

A month later, Heather and I check in by phone.

"How are you?" I ask her.

"What did you say to him?" she asks me.

I give her a general overview of our conversation, respecting Thomas' process. "How's it been at home?"

"Much better. He asks me questions. He seems more engaged than ever."

"Glad to hear that, Heather. It's not really about what I said, but Thomas' willingness to look at himself and make choices."

Prior to our meeting, Thomas had no understanding of how to engage meaningfully with himself or his partner. Heather did. With some work, he begins to understand what it means to live in his truth—to have needs, identify them, and clearly communicate them. In subsequent sessions, I introduce the idea of self-love. He soon learns that no one can love you better than yourself, because no one can know you better than yourself.

From self-love, we may have an effusive, illuminating love to offer our partner. A love that expands our light and circulates back to us. It is a love that defies contraction, free of the fear of losing each other. This is a love that asks our partner to love us as a soul ally, not a parent or a wounded child. We trust the source of the light within us instead of outsourcing it. We are in relationship with our partner and ourselves at the same time. We are two people who know the wealth of The One within ourselves. This is the you who knows you yet transcends you. From here, we may cultivate the greatest of all loves in sovereign partnership—no grasping, no resisting, free.

During times of relational fracture, we are invited to re-up our alliance and ask, *Am I in this relationship because I want it or because I fear losing it and being alone?* This ensures we are not giving ourselves away to maintain a low-quality relationship built on small love, instead of big love. We don't say, *I'd rather be loved than be me.* This is utter self-betrayal. We do not need to make such a compromise.

We can enjoy deep closeness and vivacity, connection and freedom, security and passion. It only happens when we look into the heart of what we have, what is so precious to us in union. In a sovereign relationship, we take nothing for granted and treat every interaction as sacred. We live on a plain of infinite intimacy, transcending the confining sentiments of, "You must make me safe," and entering the realm of, "Let's be in the adventure of our best selves together!"

Sovereignty in Relationship

It is often said that to find something in life, you must first know you've lost it. After twenty years in marriage, I knew I had lost my sovereignty. I did not know who I was beyond my marriage. The dream of The One became a nightmare. Having come together so young, my wife and I had never independently matured into our adult selves. The confines of so many years together, from such a young age, did more to discourage sovereignty than encourage it. While we were adults in all the ways of the outer world—work, parenting, and finances—it's fair to say that we were still children relationally.

It wasn't until my marriage ended that I experienced sovereign partnership with another woman. Sovereign partnership is one of the gifts I was able to cultivate after taking the leap. First, I had to cultivate sovereignty in my own life before I could experience it with another.

Values of Sovereign Partnership

- We seek relationship to make our lives richer and bigger, to grow and live a full path, instead of completing one another.
- We understand that a healthy self-relationship is necessary to be n healthy partnership.
- We navigate conflict lovingly.
- We are emotionally responsible *with* one another but not *for* one another.
- We trust to be emotionally safe together and always act in kindness.
- We have other important relationships and don't put everything on one another.
- We commit to take time apart and together to replenish the source of our desire.
- We have communication and congruency with our life desires and relational goals.

Sovereignty and Congruence

As my new partner and I got to know one another, I knew we shared a sovereign view of relationship. After a few bumpy attempts, we learned to navigate conflict together lovingly. In the midst of a hard conversation, we honored each other's ability to hold ourselves emotionally, supporting each other with an open heart, touch, or gaze. There was compassion, but no rescuing. With a sovereign partner, rescuing would be an affront. I could stay present with her emotions and trust that she could hold herself. If she needed help, I was a friend and not a parent. We found inter-dependence rather than co-dependence. From here, we discovered the deep trust to lean on one another.

With sovereign attributes, we could hold passion and security. We could lose ourselves in one another—fireworks and all—and still pull apart to come back to ourselves. This often meant being strong enough to feel aloneness when apart. An appreciation for solitude is a sovereign attribute, in contrast to the immature belief that *I am nothing when you are away*.

Still, from the beginning, we were in risky territory—not just because desire could overwhelm sovereignty, as it often does, but because of a core incongruence that materialized in time. She wanted a family and I did not. While we communicated openly about this from the start, achieving clarity took time. Initially, we were both open to considering a family, but in time there was clear incongruence—she, yes for family, and I, no. The strong pull of desire made it hard to uncouple as we attempted to do so multiple times.

While we both felt tears and heartbreak over many months, we did not shy away from doing what we needed to do—to part ways lovingly. Our soul contract had brought us together for the purpose to grow, as it does in all relationships. Through this lens, I could embrace the hard truth between us. I found myself thinking: *Let go of the one you love. Your grief is a reflection of your love. Love the part of you that fears letting go.* These truths helped me during a deeply sad time. And yet I took many gifts forward; for me, it was understanding the deep congruence between partners that sovereignty offers in relationship. If I can't love you the way you need to be loved in giving you a family, then I must let you go, even if it feels like it's crushing me.

The Gift of Midlife

"Life really does begin at forty. Up until then, you are just doing research."

– Attributed to Carl Jung

As we enter midlife, a sovereign relationship is more attainable. In midlife, we have a better sense of who we are, our wants and needs. The research referred to in the quote above means having lived and made mistakes.

Young people are at a disadvantage here, coming to relationship with few, if any, relationship experiences, susceptible to the spell of The One. Consider the metaphor of two half-formed entities orbiting around one another. With undeveloped core selves, they have a mutually misguided goal of becoming one. Whoever said youth is wasted on the young forgot that wisdom can be earned in middle-age.

Nonetheless, for any person, young or old, who feels the urge to lose themselves in another, I say this: Do so by all means. Enjoy the fireworks and ignite the electricity. But never forget to reclaim yourself. Always be in a healthy self-relationship. Look at your masks, shadows, and scripts. Ask, how am *I* The One? And is my partner someone with whom I share my greatest me?

Chapter 10

Falling and Getting Back Up

*"Do not judge me by my successes, judge me by how
many times I fell down and got back up again."*

– Nelson Mandela,
from an interview for the documentary Mandela

Maybe you made the leap. You spoke a hard truth that has your
relationship in shambles. Or you moved out and are living alone for
the first time ever. The axis of your life is altered. The landscape
looks different now. And everything is far from perfect. You may be
wondering: *What do I do?* That makes sense. To fall is to be human. We
all fall.

As I reconfigured my marriage, the thrill of newfound freedom could
have, at any moment, turned into a lack of purpose and loneliness. I
had made it out of the house, now what? It was easy for me to feel
lost. A dark mood might hit me like a fog bank. In a tough moment, I
would question what I'd done. How could I have left my wife? Regret
would visit me.

At times, I was troubled by these feelings. Then, in a moment of clarity,
I would realize that to think I wouldn't fall again was madness. I came

to realize that falling is part of the gift of new life. To *not* make the leap would have been the real fall. To do it and get jostled around was the thrill of the ride. We fall and enjoy the sensation as best we can. And if we get hurt, we care for ourselves, get support, and, like Mandela, get up and try again. Unlike before, we've gotten better at falling. And we are gentle with ourselves. We do less; we be more. We back off self-judgments and love ourselves. Maybe that means we're less productive. Or our energy is low. Or maybe we feel depressed. However it shows up, it's a good time to be alive.

How can we not judge that we've fallen? How can we be patient getting back up? Some days, it's just enough to get out of bed in the morning and talk with a loved one. Other days, it's marching forward through the storm, to do only what needs to get done. Conscious emancipation is not just a one off (i.e. got through the crisis, done); it is a continued stepping in.

The Emerging Relationship

Eighteen months after I had left my wife, we were still legally married. While we had no stated intention of remaining together, we were patient with our uncoupling. Twenty-five years together took some time to undo. While I was eager to move forward with my life, she asked me to wait before filing for divorce. She needed time to integrate everything, catch up with it all. From the onset, she had been devastated, trying to hold on to a part of us—something, so she could keep herself together. In asking to uncouple, I feared that I had abandoned her, but I knew better. Often, her puzzling desire for connection felt like a burden to me, but I also understood. I did my best to honor her, but was clear that I could not completely put my life on hold for her. I needed to have other experiences with other women. Having been monogamous from our early twenties to mid-forties, I was ready to experiment. Soon enough, she began dating as well.

For a period of time, we had agreed not to discuss our relationships with one another. It was a no-go zone, which created a safe space for us to reconfigure our relationship outside of marriage. Be it friendship, parenthood, or business alliance, our new relationship was unknown and emerging. We committed to doing the work of staying connected with our weekly check-ins for the well-being of our son, our business, and one another. Often, it was hard and painful, hearing truths that acknowledged the extent of our unraveling. Witnessing and listening was key; no crosstalk was allowed, and emotional safety was critical. Speaking lovingly and hearing each other's truths was important. As hard as it was at times, it was more empowering to stay connected than to completely lose twenty-five years of our lives.

For many couples going through divorce or separation, the unwillingness to be in a relationship creates a gaping black hole in their lives, a huge stretch of years that is completely lost. It's as if their time together was one big mistake that they'd prefer to forget. *How did I ever marry this person?* Self-indictment or denial often fills the gap, further etching shadow within the individual.

In divorce, most couples do not consider an emerging relationship. Instead, they just run from one another, often fighting savagely in court along the way. They have lost the opportunity to cultivate the gifts of facing sadness, regret, and shame with one another. This is understandable when adultery, physical abuse, or severe financial deception have occurred. Some betrayals require significant time and space to heal. Still, I have seen many couples come to appreciate that they came together once with much love, and would like to come apart honoring that love. That truth guided Marisa and me during our uncoupling.

With emotional maturity and resilience, we can often do better than the combative divorce. Many of us just do not know it is an option. In a heated moment, how do we pause a day or two before calling the lawyer to say, "I want you to go after everything he or she has"? Conscious uncoupling offers us the gift of our own growth, a healing of our "mistakes," an emerging relationship with our ex-spouse for the benefit of our children and families.

My wife and I were committed to maintaining our once-a-week check-ins and family dinners. Clearing the air between us, connecting one-on-one before our dinners, helped us spend time lovingly with our son as a family unit. It often felt miraculous to feel such love of family, and even laughter and joy, despite the hardships we were undergoing as a couple. Family meals helped salvage whatever relationship was emerging between us, even if it was a mere fraction of what it had once been.

So, Have You Been Seeing Someone?

One night, two weeks prior to Christmas, I asked my wife about who she was seeing. In our no-go zone agreement which we had kept for many months, I had felt a sense of false exclusivity, as if we were unconsciously holding on to a part of each another. That no longer felt right.

"So, have you been seeing someone?" I asked.

Immediately, I wanted to pull the words back into my mouth. *Do I really want to know?* I wondered. I paused and took a breath. *Yes.*

The news came. She told me that for several months she had been dating a wealthy tech entrepreneur, originally from Paris, who lived in Denver. In the last month, it had gotten more serious. They were in a "committed monogamous" relationship. To my shock, the two words put a dagger in my heart. I felt betrayed. We had agreed to date, but not monogamously. That had not been her impression, she said—and besides, it just happened. The thrill of my eighteen-month emancipation came to a sudden halt. I was stunned, realizing that I was still holding on to her.

I took a deep breath and settled with the news. *I'm okay*, I told myself. *No big deal.* And then I told a story I thought I believed.

"I'm happy for you. Romantic love feels like a box to me. I am more interested in spiritual love."

This is a win-win, I thought. *She can have her romantic love. I have spiritual love.* I expressed happiness for her, encouraging her to share more about him. I felt romantically released.

I turned to my son and said, "Mom's got a serious boyfriend."

"I know. I've met him twice," he said.

"Really?"

The Final Groundswell

A night later, I came home alone, and the news hit me for real. I knew myself well enough to know that my story to Marisa about "spiritual love" was inauthentic. I was attempting to exalt myself, but my real motive was to bypass fear and sadness. My willingness to feel those hard emotions brought out the truth. Instead of asking who she was seeing, a more sovereign way to put it would have been: "I know we are both dating, but where is it going? Are we moving toward one another or away?"

Nonetheless, I felt like a melodramatic loser, a new age spiritual bypasser. Where had all my "growth" gone? I jumped on myself pretty hard, but the self-judgments weren't getting me anywhere. I understood that the judge was really just a protector who had become overprotective to the point of harming me. Thank you, judge, job done—now, go away. Still, I couldn't deny the heartache. By setting aside the judge, I could just feel what I felt without the false shield of judgement. I recorded the following on my phone:

"The final deathblow has come to my marriage, with my beloved who I've been dancing with unconsciously. I've been having a piece of her heart still with our check-ins, even though we've been apart for some time now. I wanted to lose the old relationship we had, but I did not want to lose her. It all flashes in front of me like a kaleidoscopic dream."

I felt deeply into the fear of losing my wife. I had been the one keeping her at a distance for a year and more, creating boundaries, reconfiguring our relationship to live into my own freedom. Now, she had gone out beyond what I thought was the far wall by giving herself to another man. Now, she had a confidant. I no longer had her heart. In this, I had to face my greatest fear of being invisible like I had been as a child. I stepped in for another round of healing with the boy. *Will this ever stop?* I wondered. There was more work to be done, for him and myself. I had many friends and great support, but at the end of the day, it was me in the room with my little boy's heart. I spent the next month with him. Another major chapter in my initiatory journey of becoming whole.

I took it slow for that month, showing up for work as I could. I practiced good self-care—being with myself, writing in a journal, and committing to personal practices. I sat with my thoughts, my fears, and my breath, for as much as one to two hours and more per day. I loved myself to sleep at night with affirmations. Showing up fully with the pain was the gift. Paradoxically, I felt more alive than ever. With all of me—head, heart, body and soul—I became emancipated. My emancipation was not from my wife, but from an unintegrated part of myself: the needy child within. From there, I came alive—back into my original light with which I had been born. I became a man with the strength to embrace his soft, sweet, and loving little boy.

The Magistrate

The monogamous boyfriend proved to be a gift. It spurred me forward to do what I had to, what I had feared. I filed for divorce a few days later. At the final decree several months later, my wife and I stood together in court—just the two us, no lawyers. We had our paperwork in hand, rubber stamped by a hired financial advisor. The magistrate sat on the judicial bench like God above us. She took the documents and reviewed all the details. We waited. She looked up, glasses protruding from the tip of her nose, and questioned a component of our financial arrangement. I spoke to her concern and then Marisa, trying to demonstrate the trust we still had, said to the magistrate, "We are still loving and committed to honoring one another."

"Oh," said the magistrate. "So, you just needed to alter the structure of your relationship."

My jaw dropped, stunned at the judge's words. She got it. She said the words I'd been saying for months—alter the structure of our relationship. Yes, there was and would still be a relationship. While it was clearly the path less travelled, it was not a path untraveled. Yes, it was true. We needed to alter the structure of our relationship in order to "grow up" as healthy individuals.

And I can say today, with gratitude, that I'm so thankful we did our best to be courageous and bold along the way. We trusted that doing this our own way, even when others said we were crazy, would allow us to emerge as bigger people. In tending to ourselves, we orbited around the primary axis of all human well-being: our self-relationship.

Gratitude to My Ex-Wife

Today, my ex-wife and I remain allies. We run a business together, co-parent a teenager in college, and share details of our lives when it feels right. I want to acknowledge her as a powerful and deeply loving being. While I do not and could not know all the details of what uncoupling looked like from her perspective, I have no doubt that she has a remarkable story of her own to tell—and one day, may she tell it. From being afraid of getting on a plane to flying all over the country and ultimately to Ghana for six weeks to work in a clinic, Marisa went from devastated to transcended. She is an amazing person. And what do you know? Over time, her health even improved significantly.

And I pursued my dream of writing this book, which I completed while travelling in Spain, Mexico, and Hawaii.

In the most profound of ways, my ex-wife and I were great teachers to one another. We completed and honored our soul contract. Altering the structure of our relationship enabled its culmination. Divorce is a cruel word for such a gifted journey. Conscious uncoupling is the phrase for what we did—although in the moment, we had no idea what it was called. We were just two loving people doing our best to follow our hearts.

Chapter 11

The Gifts to Our Children

"Children are educated by what the grown-up is and not by his talk. Nothing has a stronger influence psychologically on their environment and especially on their children than the unlived life of the parent."

– Carl Jung

In the end, the path of personal growth through restructuring a marriage or relationship can feel self-involved, and it is. The soul requires it be so. As a byproduct—and more truthfully said, a main product—it offers the most profound gift to our children. That is, a healthy model of partnership.

While I often felt invisible in our family system, and felt my son was attached to his mother at the hip, the truth is I had been invisible to myself. Once I changed that, he saw me in a new way too. As he aged from fifteen to eighteen, he saw things in a new light. He grew up as well. While it was no consolation at the time, it demonstrated his new vision: "I like that you and mom are divorced. Now I get to see your side of the story." It's likely he said something similar to Marisa as well.

The point is, he came to see that two adults who love each other deeply could still love each other and dramatically change their relationship with one another. He saw what it means for his parents to come alive in a new and dramatic way and still be good to one another. At times, it is challenging to speak of the successes of our journey. It is a gift within and can be hard to put in words. Like anything that is truly sacred, it's ultimately between one's self and his or her higher power.

How do we teach our children to become healthy, emotionally mature adults? I know no better way than to be those healthy adults ourselves. In the absence of being so, what are we modeling—other than habit and fear? Understandably, we often refuse relationship change for our kids. But how does that work out? Ask the kids. So often I hear clients say years later as adults: "My parents did not have a good relationship. There was no joy in the home. I had no model of a loving relationship." Bereft of a model of loving relationship, they struggle to create one themselves. As kids, we see who our parents are; we sense their happiness or sadness. We believe ourselves somehow responsible for their feelings. It is only in adulthood that we can emancipate from the false responsibilities, claim our own experiences, and guide ourselves to a new view of the world.

And so, another great gift, among many, in taking the leap is the example you become for your children. If we come alive in life, we provide an inspired model for our children. We not only honor ourselves, but future generations as well. When we make the leap, we are heroes. The world needs more heroes. Become one, and you'll never look back.

About the Author

Stuart Motola is a master coach, author, speaker, entrepreneur, and workshop facilitator who has shared his relationship expertise throughout the world. Drawing on years of experience of coaching clients in challenged relationships and his own 20 year marriage, Stuart delivers powerful results to his clients on how to grow stronger when relationship challenges arise, particularly when the "save it or leave it" question comes up. Stuart is committed to empowering his clients to reclaim their lives so they can experience a life of freedom and fulfillment. Stuart continues to step into his desire to leave the world a better place for his son and all those he touches.

Connect with the Author

Website: www.StuartMotola.com

Email: info@StuartMotola.com

Social Media:

Facebook:
https://www.facebook.com/StuartMotolaCoaching/

LinkedIn:
https://www.linkedin.com/in/stuart-motola-20812b1/

Twitter: @StuartMotola

Youtube:
https://www.youtube.com/user/stuartmotola

Acknowledgements

Fixing You Is Killing Me would not have been possible without the steady and inspiring guidance of my editor, James Churches. Throughout the writing process, James consistently coached me on how to craft the narrative arc of this book. Not just my editor, James has also been a great ally, with whom I've had the pleasure to journey for over fifteen years. He knew this book was important to my own growth, as well as that of my readers. Thank you, James. It's been quite a ride. Reign in the horse!

Thanks to Rick Killian for his help on the book title, and Chantal Pierrat for her help on the subtitle.

Special thanks to my dear friend Nick who stood by me, step by step, during the time of my uncoupling.

Gratitude to Michelle for being a great ally in this life.

Endless thanks to my mom for her love and continued belief in me.

And to all who remain unnamed and have touched my path. You are my copilots. I am blessed to have you in my life.

References

Alighieri, Dante. *Inferno, Canto I*, 1320.

Baba, Prem. *From Suffering to Joy: The Path of the Heart.* New York: SelectBooks, 2013.

Beecher, Willard, and Marguerite Beecher. *Beyond Success and Failure: Ways to Self-Reliance and Maturity.* The Julian Press, Inc., 1966.

Bly, Robert, James Hillman, and Michael Meade. *The Rag and Bone Shop of the Heart: A Poetry Anthology.* New York: Harper Collins, 1993.

Brach, Tara. "Tara Brach." Audio blog post, 2017.

Buck, Chris, and Jennifer Lee, dir. *Frozen.* Walt Disney Animation Studios, 2013. DVD.

Campbell, Joseph. *The Hero with a Thousand Faces.* Princeton: Princeton University Press, 1968.

Campbell, Joseph. "The Wisdom of Joseph Campbell." Interviews with Michael Toms. *New Dimensions (Audio Series).* Recorded 1975-1987. Originally broadcast 1990. Re-released Hay House, 2005.

Douglas, Frederick. "Abolitionist Meeting." Public Speech, New Bedford Massachusetts, 1855.

Garvey, Marcus. "Speech at Menelik Hall." Sidney, Novia Scotia, 1937.

Gibson, Angus, and Jo Menell, dir. *Mandela.* Island Pictures, 1996. DVD.

Gilbert, Elizabeth. *Eat, Pray, Love: One Woman's Search for Everything Across Italy, India and Indonesia.* London: Penguin Books, 2006.

Gillette, Douglas, and Robert Moore. *The King Within: Accessing the King in the Male Psyche.* Exploration Press, 1992.

Gurian, Michael. *The Invisible Presence: How a Man's Relationship with His Mother Affects All His Relationships with Women (2nd Revised Edition)*. Boston: Shambhala, 2010.

Hendrix, Harville. *Getting the Love You Want*. Melbourne: Schwartz and Wilkinson, 1988.

Johnson, Robert. *Owning Your Own Shadow: Understanding the Dark Side of the Psyche*. New York: HarperOne, 1991.

Jung, Carl. *Memories, Dreams, Reflections*. New York: Crown Publishing Group/Random House, 1963.

Jung, Carl. *The Philosophical Tree*. Collected Works 13, Alchemical Studies. Princeton: Princeton University Press, 1967.

Kahn, Matt. "Soul Contracts, Twin Flames and Soul Mates Redefined." YouTube Video, 1:31. July 8, 2015.

Klein, Joey. *The Inner Matrix: A Guide to Transforming Your Life and Awakening Your Spirit*. Bloomington: Balboa Press, 2014.

Kübler-Ross, Elisabeth. *On Death and Dying: What the Dying Have to Teach Doctors, Nurses, Clergy, and Their Own Families*. New York: The Macmillan Company, 1969.

Kurr van Gennep, Charles-Arnold. *The Rites of Passage*. Chicago: University of Chicago Press, 1909.

Lesser, Elizabeth. *Broken Open: How Difficult Times Can Help Us Grow*. New York: Villard, 2005.

Mandela, Nelson. *Long Walk to Freedom: The Autobiography of Nelson Mandela*. New York: Back Bay Books, 1995.

Meade, Michael. *Fate and Destiny, the Two Agreements of the Soul*. Greenfire Press, 2004.

Nguyen, Viet Thanh. *The Sympathizer*. New York: Grove Press, 2015.

Nietzsche, Friedrich. *Beyond Good and Evil*. New York: Vintage, 1989.

Marley, Bob and The Wailers. *Redemption Song.* "Uprising." Island/Tuff Gong, 1980.

Nin, Anais. *Delta of Venus.* London: W H Allen, 1977.

Palmer, Parker. *A Hidden Wholeness: The Journey Toward an Undivided Life.* San Francisco: Jossey-Bass, 2004.

Perel, Esther. *Mating in Captivity: Unlocking Erotic Intelligence.* New York: Harper Collins, 2006.

Pierrakos, Eva. *The Pathwork of Self-Transformation.* New York: Bantam, 1990.

Pressfield, Steven. *The War of Art: Break Through the Blocks and Win Your Inner Creative Battles.* New York: Warner Books, 2002.

Prince and The Revolution. *I Would Die 4 U.* "Purple Rain." Warner Brothers, 1984.

Real, Terry. "New Rules for Couples." REAL Relational Solutions. www.terryreal.com.

Rohr, Richard. *Falling Upward: A Spirituality for the Two Halves of Life.* San Francisco: Jossey-Bass, 2011.

Rumi, Jalalludin. "Who Says Words with My Mouth?" In *The Book of Love: Poems of Ecstasy and Longing.* New York: HarperOne, 2005.

Samples, Bob. *Metaphoric Mind: A Celebration of Creative Consciousness.* Fawnskin: Jalmar Press, 1993.

Sebastiana, Dene Maria. Sun Moon Coaching. www.sunmooncoaching.com.

Sigmund, Freud. *Beyond the Pleasure Principle.* London: International Psycho-Analytical, 1920.

Stevens, Cat. *Father and Son.* "Tea for The Tillerman." Island, 1970.

Talking Heads. *Once in a Lifetime.* "Remain In Light." Sire, 1981.

Tashiro, Ty. *The Science of Happily Ever After.* Ontario: Harlequin, 2014.

The Beatles. *All You Need Is Love. Single.* "Parlophone." Capitol, 1967.

The Clash. *Should I Stay or Should I Go?* "Combat Rock." Epic Records, 1982.

Trungpa, Chögyam. *Smile at Fear: Awakening the True Heart of Bravery.* Boston: Shambhala, 2010.

Williamson, Marianne. *A Return to Love: Reflections on the Principles of "A Course in Miracles."* New York: Harper Collins, 1992.

Williams, Terry Tempest. *When Women Were Birds: Fifty-four Variations on Voice.* New York: Sarah Crichton Books, 2012.